Writing Better

Writing Better

Effective Strategies for Teaching Students with Learning Difficulties

by

Steve Graham, Ed.D.

and

Karen R. Harris, Ed.D.

Vanderbilt University
Nashville, Tennessee

·P A U L·H·
BROOKES
PUBLISHING C<u>O</u> ®

Baltimore • London • Sydney

Paul H. Brookes Publishing Co.
Post Office Box 10624
Baltimore, Maryland 21285-0624

www.brookespublishing.com

Typeset by Auburn Associates, Inc., Baltimore, Maryland.
Manufactured in the United States of America by
Versa Press, Inc., East Peoria, Illinois.

The vignettes in this book are composites based on the authors' experiences. In all instances,
names and identifying details have been changed to protect confidentiality.

Library of Congress Cataloging-in-Publication Data

Graham, Steven, 1950–
 Writing better: effective strategies for teaching students with learning
 difficulties / by Steve Graham and Karen R. Harris.
  p.   cm.
 Includes bibliographical references and index.
 ISBN 1-55766-704-7 (pbk.)
 1. English language—Composition and exercises—Study and teaching.
 2. Learning disabled children—Education.   I. Harris, Karen R. II. Title.

LB1576 .G7254 2005
808'.042'071—dc22   2004029490

British Library Cataloguing in Publication data are available from the British Library.

Contents

About the Authors

Steve Graham, Ed.D., is Professor and the Currey-Ingram Chair in Special Education at Vanderbilt University, Nashville, Tennessee. He is the current editor of *Exceptional Children* and the past editor of *Contemporary Educational Psychology*. He is the co-author of the *Handbook of Learning Disabilities; Making the Writing Process Work: Strategies for Composition and Self-Regulation; Teaching Every Child Every Day: Learning in Diverse Schools and Classrooms; Teaching Every Adolescent Every Day; Spell It–Write* (a spelling program for children in grades K through 9); and the upcoming *Handbook of Writing Research*. Dr. Graham's research has focused mainly on identifying the factors that contribute to the development of writing difficulties; the development and validation of effective procedures for teaching planning, revising, and the mechanics of writing to struggling writers; and the use of technology to enhance writing performance and development.

Karen R. Harris, Ed.D., is Professor and the Currey-Ingram Chair in Special Education at Vanderbilt University, Nashville, Tennessee. She has taught kindergarten and fourth-grade students, as well as elementary and secondary students with disabilities. She is co-author, with Steve Graham, of the books *Making the Writing Process Work: Strategies for Composition and Self-Regulation; Teaching Every Child Every Day: Learning in Diverse Schools and Classrooms; Handbook of Learning Disabilities;* and the curriculum *Spell It–Write.* Dr. Harris is the editor of the *Journal of Educational Psychology.* Her research is focused on theoretical and intervention issues in the development of academic and self-regulation strategies among students with attention-deficit/hyperactivity disorder, learning disabilities, and other challenges.

Writing Better

The Power of Writing

Writing is one of humankind's most powerful tools. Its mastery is essential for success both in and out of school. Among other things, writing

- Allows people to communicate with others who are removed by distance and time

- Makes it possible to gather, preserve, and transmit information widely

- Offers a powerful tool for refining and extending one's knowledge about a topic

- Provides a flexible medium for artistic, political, spiritual, and self-expression (Applebee, 1984; Diamond, 1999; Durst & Newell, 1989; Graham & Harris, 2000a)

Writing can even have therapeutic effects because writing about one's feelings can lower blood pressure, reduce depression, and boost the immune system (Swedlow, 1999).

The purpose of this book is to help students with learning disabilities, as well as other struggling writers, harness the power of writing. Skilled writing is strategic. Good writers use a variety of strategies to help them manage the writing process and to create and improve what they write (Hayes & Flower, 1986; Zimmerman & Reisemberg, 1997). Strategies for writing include planning, monitoring, evaluating, and revising text. Struggling writers, including those with learning disabilities, employ an approach to writing that minimizes the use of these processes (Graham, 1990; McCutchen, 1988; Scardamalia & Bereiter, 1986; Thomas, Englert, & Gregg, 1987). We believe that this problem is best tackled head-on by explicitly teaching these children the same kinds of strategies used by their more skilled counterparts. This book contains a variety of scientifically validated writing strategies that are appropriate for elementary-age students. These strategies are briefly summarized in Table I.1, which includes strategies for regulating the writing process (self-monitoring and goal setting) and strategies for planning and revising text. Strategies that can be applied with different types or genres of writing are listed first in Table I.1, followed by strategies designed for a particular type of writing (e.g., story telling).

It is important to note that all of the strategies presented in this book were validated in one or more scientific studies involving children with learning disabilities (see

Table I.1. Scientifically validated writing strategies

Strategy	Description	Genre	It Helps the Writer	Location
Self-monitor and record writing output	Count and graph the number of words written in each paper	All genres	Generate content Sustain attention	Chapter 15
PLEASE	Plan and write a paragraph containing a topic sentence, supporting details, and a concluding statement	All genres	Generate content Organize content Evaluate content Write a paragraph	Chapter 4
PLANS	Plan and write a paper by determining what it will include once it is completed	All genres	Plan in advance Set writing goals Generate content Write a complete paper	Chapter 5
STOP and LIST	Plan and write a paper by setting goals, brainstorming, and sequencing ideas	All genres	Plan in advance Set writing goals Generate content Evaluate content Write a complete paper	Chapter 6
Summary writing	Summarize reading material in writing by identifying main idea and important points	All genres	Identify important information Plan in advance Organize content Evaluate content Write a complete summary	Chapter 9
Set a goal for revising	Revise a paper by setting a goal to add three or more ideas to it	All genres	Generate content Revise by adding text	Chapter 16
Peer revising	Revise and edit a paper after receiving feedback from a peer on its substance and form	All genres	Revise for clarity Revise by adding text Edit for spelling, punctuation, and sentence errors	Chapter 7
CDO	Revise a paper by using specific criteria to evaluate and modify each sentence	All genres	Revise sentences for clarity, intention, interest, and believability	Chapter 8
Self-monitor and record story parts	Count and graph the number of basic story parts included in each story	Story	Generate content Write a complete story	Chapter 15

Strategy	Description	Genre	Components	Chapter
Vocabulary	Plan and write a story by brainstorming action and describing words to use in it	Story	Plan in advance Generate content	Chapter 10
Story grammar	Plan and write a story by brainstorming ideas for each part of the story before writing it	Story	Plan in advance Generate content Organize content Write a complete story	Chapter 10
Set general and elaborated goals	Plan and write a persuasive paper by setting a general goal to persuade the reader that your position is correct; set elaborated goals to include a clear premise, give reasons and examples to support the premise, and refute reasons for the other side of the argument	Persuasion	Generate content Write a complete essay	Chapter 16
Three-step strategy with TREE	Plan and write a persuasive paper by brainstorming ideas for each part of the essay before writing it	Persuasion	Plan in advance Set writing goals Generate content Organize content Evaluate content Write a complete essay	Chapter 11
STOP and DARE	Plan and write a persuasive paper by brainstorming ideas for each part of the essay before writing it; evaluate if each part of the paper is included	Persuasion	Plan in advance Set writing goal Generate content Organize content Evaluate content Write a complete essay	Chapter 11
SCAN	Revise a persuasive paper by strengthening support for the premise, adding needed information, checking each sentence for clarity and cohesiveness, and correcting spelling and other errors	Persuasion	Revise for clarity Revise for coherence Revise by adding text Evaluate content Correct spelling and other errors Write a complete essay	Chapter 11
POWER strategy: Explanations	Plan, write, and revise an informative paper by brainstorming and organizing possible ideas before writing it; revise the paper with the help of a peer to ensure that it is clear, interesting, and complete	Explanation	Plan in advance Set writing goal Generate content Organize content Revise for clarity, interest, and completeness	Chapter 12

(continued)

Table I.1. *(continued)*

Strategy	Description	Genre	It Helps the Writer	Location
POWER strategy: Comparison/contrast	Plan, write, and revise a comparison/contrast paper by brainstorming and organizing possible ideas before writing it; revise the paper with the help of a peer to ensure that it is clear, interesting, and complete	Comparison/ contrast	Plan in advance Set writing goal Generate content Organize content Revise for clarity, interest, and completeness	Chapter 13
Report writing	Plan and write a report by brainstorming and gathering additional information from other sources, organizing the collected information on a web, deciding what information to use and the order of its presentation, and checking to be sure the report is complete	Report	Plan in advance Generate content Gather content Organize content Evaluate content Write a complete report	Chapter 14

Graham, in press). Thus, there is evidence that they work with these children. Writing strategy instruction has been successful not only with struggling writers but also with good and average writers (Graham & Harris, 2003a). It makes the formidable tasks of planning, revising, and regulating the writing process more concrete. This is beneficial for young writers. Writing strategy instruction provides children with the tools they need to be better writers—writers who are strategic can plan effectively and are reflective.

HOW THE BOOK UNFOLDS

In Section I, we begin our exploration of writing strategy instruction by examining why it is an important ingredient in learning to write. This involves determining what strategies are and why learning to use them is a good idea. We then consider what is currently known about the writing behaviors of students with learning disabilities. This includes examining difficulties these children have with persistence, planning, idea generation, organizing text, and revising. These same difficulties are also experienced by students without learning disabilities who find writing difficult (Graham & Harris, 2002).

Section II introduces a scientifically validated model for teaching writing strategies (Graham & Harris, 2003a). This model is *self-regulated strategy development instruction*, which has been used to teach the majority of the strategies included in this book. It is designed to help students learn how to apply writing strategies independently, effectively, and thoughtfully. The application of the model is illustrated with three examples from real-life situations. They show how to implement the model to teach writing strategies in an inclusive classroom, in a small group setting, and in one-to-one tutoring.

The next three sections of the book present scientifically validated writing strategies that are designed to address the problems experienced by students with learning disabilities. In Section III, strategies are introduced for planning, writing, and revising that can be applied broadly to any writing genre. We have included strategies for planning and writing a paragraph, a complete paper, and a summary of material. Section III also includes strategies for revising and editing text independently or in conjunction with a peer. In contrast, Section IV focuses on strategies designed for a specific genre. We include planning, writing, and revising strategies for composing stories, expressing opinions, providing explanations, comparing and contrasting, and developing a report. In Section V, two strategies for regulating writing and the writing process are examined: self-monitoring and recording of writing performance and goal setting.

A common format is used to present each writing strategy in Chapters 4–16. First, the strategy is introduced by describing its purpose and the steps for executing it. Second, procedures for teaching the strategy are examined, including tips for making instruction more effective. Third, the scientific evidence validating the use of the strategy with students with learning disabilities is presented. This evidence is shared in a teacher-friendly form, and the children participating in the validating study are described. This format allows teachers to examine the potential power of the strategy and determine how to use it with the children in their classrooms. Fourth, other groups of students who would likely benefit from learning the strategy are identified. Finally, suggestions on how the strategy can be modified and extended are explored.

The last section of this book concentrates on how to make writing strategy instruction work in the classroom. We include practical advice on getting started, creating a supportive learning environment, and evaluating the implementation and impact of teaching writing strategies.

Throughout the book, we draw on the insights and wisdom of professional writers, the wit and whimsy of children, and the humorous but thoughtful creations of cartoonists. The sources for cartoons, quotations, or ideas produced by professional writers and children are not presented in text but are listed at the end of the book. All other sources are cited in text, with a full reference list at the end of the book.

CHAPTER 1

Writing Uphill

Why Strategy Instruction Is Important

Writers love poking fun at their chosen profession while exalting the demanding nature of their work. The French novelist Peter De Vries once quipped, "I love writing. It's the paperwork that gets me." Red Smith grumbled, "Writing is easy. All you have to do is sit down at a typewriter and open a vein." Stephen Leacock claimed, "Writing is no trouble, just jot down ideas as they occur to you. The jotting is simplicity itself—it is the occurring which is difficult." Even the venerable Dr. Seuss found writing difficult, complaining that "every sentence is like a pang of birth. *The Cat in the Hat* ended up taking well over a year."

Children also recognize that writing presents unique challenges. When asked what is the hardest thing about being a writer, one youngster observed, "That's easy. Your hands always hurt from writing so much." Another child viewed writing as an almost impossible task, noting, "I'd like to be an author, but you have to be dead."

Although writing is a demanding task, it is not an impossible one. Many children grow up to be good writers, and some eventually pursue careers as professional writers. A fairly large number of children, however, experience difficulty mastering this basic skill. Evaluations done as part of the National Assessment of Educational Progress indicated that only one of every five high school seniors acquires the writing knowledge and skills needed at their respective grade level (Greenwald, Persky, Cambell, & Mazzeo, 1999; Persky, Daane, & Jin, 2003). The writing of an equal number of students is so poor that they have not even partially mastered these skills. These struggling writers and their younger counterparts would likely empathize with Charlie Brown, the popular character in the *Peanuts* cartoon strip, who tells his pen pal that sometimes it feels like he is writing uphill.

Why do these children write so poorly? One reason is that they do not use the same types of writing strategies as youngsters who are good writers. For example, when we asked good writers to tell us what they do when they write, the overwhelming majority of their responses focused on generating and organizing ideas for writing, reading and evaluating written text, editing and revising it, and monitoring the writing process (Graham, Schwartz, & MacArthur, 1993). As one fifth grader succinctly put it, "Good writers brainstorm ideas . . . then think about it and write it . . . look it over to see how to make it right . . . then they do a final copy and go over that; and then, if it is still not right, they do it again." In contrast, struggling writers were much less likely to identify these same processes, focusing more of their attention on the physical act of producing text. When we asked one young man to tell us the keys to good writing, he responded, "Write big to fill up the paper." Another struggling writer told us to "make it neat and check the spelling."

The responses of these children were consistent with other investigations showing that struggling writers spend less time planning (McCutchen, 1995), make fewer revisions (Fitzgerald, 1987; MacArthur, Graham, & Harris, 2004), and are less knowledgeable about writing strategies than their peers who write better (Englert, Raphael, Fear, & Anderson, 1988). Even more compelling, teachers can improve the performance of struggling writers, especially those with learning disabilities, by teaching them specific writing strategies. This includes strategies for planning and writing a paper, revising text, monitoring the writing processes, and managing the composition task (De La Paz, Swanson, & Graham, 1998; Graham & Harris, 1996; Harris & Graham, 1999; Zimmerman & Reisemberg, 1997). Taken together, these findings indicate that children's difficulties with writing are caused, at least in part, by problems acquiring, using, or managing writing strategies (Graham & Harris, 2000b).

The most direct way to address this problem is to systematically teach children the tools they need to carry out the planning, revising, and other writing processes so critical to effective writing. This is especially important for children with learning disabilities, as there is a considerable amount of scientific evidence that demonstrates that they do not acquire a variety of learning strategies unless detailed and explicit instruction is provided (Brown & Campione, 1990). Teachers can improve these children's writing by helping them acquire the same types of writing strategies used by more skilled writers. This includes strategies for planning and revising text as well as strategies for managing writing behaviors and the process of writing. Teaching students these strategies makes the task of writing more concrete and less formidable, making writing less of an uphill battle for these children.

WHAT IS A STRATEGY?

A *strategy* is a set of operations or actions that a person consciously undertakes in order to accomplish a desired goal (Alexander, Graham, & Harris, 1998). One of the most basic attributes of a strategy is that it involves purposeful behavior. This includes consciously deciding that a course of action is needed to meet a desired goal. For example, a young girl who was asked to write about the person she most admired decided to make the topic of her paper about her mother (desired goal). She picked a slightly unusual course of action, however, when she asked her mom to "tell me some of the things that I most admire about you."

A strategy also involves the "how to" or procedural knowledge needed to accomplish the desired goal. For example, a child who wanted to realize his goal of fooling his teacher into thinking he was paying attention needed to know how to paint open eyes on his glasses to make his goal a reality. Strategic know-how can take the form of a step-by-step technique for accomplishing a specific objective. In writing, this may include knowledge about how to write a paragraph (e.g., begin with a topic sentence, follow with one or more sentences that provide supporting details or examples) or how to write a certain type of poem, such as a haiku. Procedural knowledge can also consist of more general guidelines, such as the advice given to beginning reporters to include information about who, what, when, where, why, and how when describing an event. Step-by-step procedures are more commonly used when the task or problem is well-defined, whereas general guidelines are more likely to be used to solve ill-defined or ill-structured writing tasks.

Two other attributes of a strategy are highlighted in a *Calvin and Hobbes* cartoon in which Calvin tells his imaginary stuffed tiger friend, Hobbes, that he has a strategy for tackling hard problems like reading an entire chapter in his history book. He goes on to explain that the secret is to break the task down into manageable chunks and deal with each chunk one step at a time. Although he clearly has a workable plan, he tosses the book aside stating that the first step is to ask yourself if you care enough to make the effort. As Calvin's behavior demonstrates, strategies involve more than just a goal, plan, and know-how. They require the will to embark on the designated course of action and the effort to see it through. Intentions and know-how have to be paired with will and effort for writing strategies to be effective.

Strategies, therefore, are purposeful, procedural, willful, and effortful. They include a procedure or plan for accomplishing a desired objective. They must also be deliberately activated and require commitment and effort to be effective.

WHY STRATEGY INSTRUCTION IS A GOOD IDEA

Louis L'Amour, a popular writer of western novels, noted, "A writer's brain is like a magician's hat. If you're going to get anything out of it, you have to put something in first." Part of what teachers need to help children put in is strategic know-how. Strategies are essential to attaining competence. No one can become a skilled writer without learning how to gain access to, organize, and transform information and how to regulate writing processes and behaviors (Alexander et al., 1998).

That is not to say that strategic knowledge is needed for every writing task. Many of the writing tasks that occur as a part of everyday life, such as writing reminders or a note to a friend, do not usually require a strategic solution or a great deal of effort. This is not the case for many of the more important writing assignments children encounter at school. Writing a report, crafting a story, or drafting an essay are not easy or routine tasks. Such assignments typically benefit from a deliberate, systematic, and strategic approach.

How does teaching writing strategies to students with learning disabilities help them and other struggling writers complete these kinds of tasks and become better writers? First, a strategy specifies a course of action for successfully completing the writing assignment or some part of it. This helps children organize and sequence their behavior when carrying out a particular process or task. Consider the process of revising. To make a revision, a writer must first recognize that a change is needed (e.g., the text doesn't sound right at this point). The writer then identifies what is causing the problem (e.g., the sentence is not complete) and determines the kind of change needed to correct it (e.g., add a subject). The revision is then executed (Bereiter & Scardamalia, 1982). These discrete actions may not happen consistently or at all for struggling writers because they have difficulty directing their attention to the appropriate action at the proper time (Graham, 1997). Teachers can correct this problem by teaching students a strategy or routine that ensures that the separate actions involved in revising are activated and occur in an organized or regular fashion.

A second advantage of teaching writing strategies to students is that the mental operations that occur during composing are made visible and concrete. A writer's strategic behavior is typically hidden from view, as it occurs in the mind. When teachers model how to use a writing strategy, they make these mental actions more transparent by demonstrating verbally and visually how to do them. This also helps make relatively abstract processes, such as generating ideas for writing, more tangible. For example, when teachers model how to generate possible writing content or ideas via a strategy such as brainstorming, they typically specify the rules for using this procedure. These may include an edict that evaluation is suspended during brainstorming, and an "anything goes" policy is adopted when generating possible ideas. These rules provide structure and establish guidelines for brainstorming, making it less abstract and more concrete.

A third benefit of teaching writing strategies to students is that struggling writers learn new methods for composing. Learning new tools for planning, revising, or regulating the writing process is critical for these children. Contemporary approaches to writing instruction, such as the highly popular Writer's Workshop, for example, stress the use of predictable routines for writing, as students are encouraged to plan, draft, edit, revise, and publish their written work. Surprisingly little attention is devoted to explicitly teaching these processes (Graham & Harris, 1997a). Instead, many teachers who use this approach rely heavily on informal learning procedures to promote strategic development. They assume that the needed know-how will be acquired naturally, as children write for real purposes in a supportive environment. Although these teachers typically provide some direct assistance in learning writing strategies through mini-lessons, writing conferences, or teachable moments, this assistance often consists of hints, questions, or tactful responding aimed at promoting discovery of useful strategies (Freedman, 1993). Such instruction is not explicit or strong enough for most struggling writers, especially those with learning disabilities (Graham & Harris, 1997b).

Strategy instruction can also maximize struggling writers' use of the computer as a medium for composing, especially for revising. One of the most powerful features of word processing, for example, is that text can be added, altered, moved, or deleted without tedious recopying. Students with learning disabilities often fail to take advantage of this editing feature, as their basic approach to revising involves correcting mechanical miscues and making simple word changes (Harris & Graham, 1996). Teaching them a strategy that focuses their attention on larger and more substantive problems, however, can result in greater use of the editing features of word processing, as they are more likely to add ideas and rewrite parts of their text (Graham & MacArthur, 1988).

Another benefit of teaching writing strategies to students is that it enhances their knowledge about writing, the writing process, and their capabilities as writers (Graham & Harris, 1993). When struggling writers are taught a strategy for planning a story, for example, they acquire information on the content and structure of stories, as well as procedural knowledge on how to generate and organize possible ideas for writing. As they use the writing strategy, they obtain additional information on the value of the strategy and their competence as a writer (Zimmerman & Risemberg, 1997). If the strategy improves performance, it will likely have a salutary effect on students' confidence or sense of efficacy for writing. Enhanced efficacy, in turn, can boost motivation for writing, increase effort, and serve as a catalyst for more strategic behavior. In this sense, writing strategies not only influence immediate performance but also contribute to a student's overall writing development (Scardamalia & Bereiter, 1985a).

Although teaching writing strategies to students with learning disabilities can improve their performance, change how they approach the task of composing, increase writing knowledge, enhance self-efficacy, and boost motivation, it is not a panacea. Writing strategy instruction does not encompass all of the skills that children need to learn to become effective writers. This includes, but is not limited to, mastering handwriting, spelling, capitalization, punctuation, sentence construction, the rules of usage, and the stylistic conventions of different genres. Young writers also need to become familiar with the various functions of writing, develop a rich writing vocabulary, gain an appreciation of their audience, and acquire a writing voice. Developing strategic know-how is essential, but struggling writers must obtain other skills and knowledge as well. As a result, strategy instruction cannot replace the writing program but should be an integral part of it.

CHAPTER 2

Writing Is a Dog's Life

A Guide to Writing Difficulties

In the summer of 1965, a then unknown writer carried his typewriter to the top of his house and began a long, but not always distinguished, writing career. Although this author never published a single work, his writing has entertained millions for decades. The first seven words that he typed—"It was a dark and stormy night"—were synonymous with bad writing. Who was this paragon of literature? Of course, it was Snoopy, the beloved dog from the comic strip *Peanuts*.

Snoopy enjoyed a rich fantasy life, involving many careers and personas ranging from litigious lawyer to hapless scout master to World War I flying ace. Through Snoopy and the other *Peanuts* characters, Charles Schulz captured many of the nuisances and intricacies of childhood. Perhaps because he was a writer himself, many of his cartoons focused on the act of writing: Charlie Brown writing to his pen pal, his sister Sally composing letters to Santa Claus, and Peppermint Patty winning the city writing contest (even though she was a perennial D− student). None of Schulz's characters captured the complexities and difficulties of writing better than Snoopy, however. He serves as our guide, as we examine the writing of children with learning disabilities and other struggling writers.

APPROACH TO WRITING

Sitting on top of his doghouse, typewriter at paw, Snoopy writes a sentence about how the mist is turning to rain. He pauses and types a sentence about the rain turning to snow. After another pause, he types that his story is becoming dull, whereupon he throws his paper away.

Children with learning disabilities use a similar technique when they write. They compose by creating or drawing from memory a relevant idea, writing it down, and using each preceding phrase or sentence to stimulate the next idea (Graham, 1990; Thomas, Englert, & Gregg, 1987). This approach was evident in this short essay written by a fifth-grade child with a learning disability: "I think they should know how to speak different languages. If they go to like Dutch country, somebody might ask them something. They could have two kinds of language." In this case, the child was asked to write an essay on whether children his age should learn a foreign language.

This approach to writing is aptly named knowledge-telling and is primarily dominated by a single composing process, the generation of content (Scardamalia & Bereiter, 1986). Information that is somewhat topic appropriate is created or retrieved from memory and turned into written language. Little attempt is made to evaluate or rework these ideas or to consider the constraints imposed by the topic, the needs of the audience, or the organization of text (McCutchen, 1988). The resulting paper is typically a list of topic-related ideas, instead of a well-organized coherent discussion of the topic. This retrieve-and-write process simplifies the task of writing by eliminating the development of rhetorical goals and minimizes the use of planning, monitoring, evaluating, revising, and other self-regulatory strategies. Unlike skilled writing, which is well planned and reflective, the knowledge-telling approach functions much like an automated and forward-moving content generation program. Such an approach is not especially effective for tasks such as writing an essay, a report, or a story. These writing tasks typically require more than just generating or retrieving ideas on the fly. A good story, for example, includes a plot, is organized in a logical manner, and must capture the interest of the intended audience. Producing a good story requires forethought and planning, as well as reflection.

Planning in Advance

> While writing his life story, Snoopy indicates that soon after he was born, he was adopted by a kid with a round head (also known as Charlie Brown). When Lucy tells him that he should use his owner's name, he shrugs it off because he hates doing all of that research.

Children with learning disabilities do not spend much time planning their papers in advance (Graham, Harris, MacArthur, & Schwartz, 1991). Instead, they mostly plan what they are going to say while they write. Much of this planning is episodic, with each preceding idea serving as the stimulus for the next one. In contrast, skilled writers often spend a considerable amount of time planning before and while they write, developing goals to guide what they do and say (Hayes & Flower, 1986).

Even when students with learning disabilities are asked directly to plan in advance, they spend little time engaged in this activity. For example, when we prompted fifth- and sixth-grade children with learning disabilities to plan before writing, they averaged less than 1 minute of advanced planning time (MacArthur & Graham, 1987). When they do plan in advance, their plans often resemble a first draft, consisting of a series of sentences that are just rewritten during the drafting phase of writing (Graham & Harris, 1989b).

Generating Content

While working on another section of his memoirs, Snoopy writes of the constant struggle that has been his life. When Lucy laughs at this, he adds her laughter to his paper. Although this addition is ill-advised, it is not surprising, as Snoopy is constantly struggling to find something to say.

Children with learning disabilities experience similar difficulties in generating ideas for their compositions. One of the most striking characteristics of their writing is that they produce so little of it. Their stories and essays are inordinately short, containing little elaboration or detail, and once an idea is generated, they are very reluctant to discard it (Graham et al., 1991). This stands in stark contrast to skilled writers who frequently generate more than they need and must eliminate unneeded ideas or information.

The brevity of struggling writers' compositions is illustrated in these two compositions produced by a third-grade child with a learning disability. Each is incomplete and contains little detail.

Once upon a time there lived two dogs named Mack, and the other dog named Mack. And the little Mack wanted to go fishing. The big Mack liked to go fish and they lived happily ever after. [Story]

I think children should choose their own pet, because whatever pet they like their mother can get for them. [Essay written in response to the prompt "Should children be allowed to choose their own pets?"]

Why do these children write so little? One explanation is that teachers ask them to write about topics that they know little about. Even when teachers ask them to write as much as they can about familiar topics, however, they usually produce little content. The same third-grade child produced this brief composition when asked to write about his favorite place: "My favorite place is where you can play and eat. Also, it has good things you can play on. And it has candy. And you can win toys."

A more likely reason why these children produce so little content is that they have trouble gaining access to what they do know. We found that output doubled or even tripled when students with learning disabilities were prompted three times to write more about an assigned topic (Graham, 1990). We further found that the length of these students' stories increased threefold when they were asked to dictate rather than write or type their compositions (MacArthur & Graham, 1987). These children commonly know more than what they write.

Persistence

> As Snoopy is working on a story, Lucy informs him that it took Leo Tolstoy
> 6 years to write *War and Peace*. Snoopy thoughtfully reflects that he
> knows just how Tolstoy felt—he had been toiling away on his story for
> more than half an hour.

Children with learning disabilities also devote little time or effort to their writing. When we asked children with learning disabilities ages 10–12 to write an essay expressing their opinions on a specific topic, for example, they typically spent 6 minutes or less writing their paper (Graham, 1990).

When we examined the content of the persuasive essays written by students with learning disabilities ages 10–12, it was clear that they had stopped the composing process too soon. Their essays commonly began with either a "yes" or "no," followed by one or two brief reasons, abruptly ending without a resolution or concluding statement. Others have noted that children with learning disabilities experience difficulty sustaining their thinking about a topic, as evidenced by their difficulty in producing multiple statements about familiar subjects (Thomas et al., 1987). This suggests that a lack of sustained effort is more than just a problem with motivation. It may also be influenced by a child's skills in carrying out other important writing processes, such as content generation.

Revising

> After Snoopy writes about a gunshot ringing out on a dark and stormy
> night, an exasperated Lucy berates him and asks him why he can't write
> about nice things. Snoopy immediately changes *gunshot* to *kiss*.

This is a common interaction between Snoopy, the writer, and Lucy, the editor, with Lucy critiquing some aspect of his writing and Snoopy responding by making a revision that has either no effect or makes little sense. Students with learning disabilities adopt a similar technique when revising. They employ a thesaurus approach, focusing most of their efforts on making word substitutions, correcting errors involving spelling and usage, and producing a neater product (MacArthur & Graham, 1987; MacArthur, Graham, & Schwartz, 1991). This is due to the large number of spelling, capitalization, punctuation, and other errors they make when writing; their belief that revising equals proofreading; and their lack of effective strategies for making more substantive revisions (Graham & Harris, 2003a).

In contrast to the extensive modifications made by skilled writers (Fitzgerald, 1987), less than 20% of the revisions made by children with learning disabilities change what they had written (MacArthur et al., 1991). Perhaps even more important, two thirds of these changes have either a neutral or negative effect on text. For example, one child told us that he changed "he *loved* farm work" to "he *liked* farm work" (a neutral change) because the reader probably would not understand why the main character "loves farm work" (Graham, 1997). Another child indicated that he deleted three sentences that were central to understanding his story (a negative change) because "people won't care about that part."

The majority of revisions made by struggling writers involve minor changes in the surface level features of text (MacArthur & Graham, 1987; MacArthur, Graham, & Schwartz, 1991). More than 70% of these changes are attempts to correct capitalization, punctuation, spelling, format, and so forth. Like the content changes these students make, their attempts to correct these errors are generally ineffective. There is no significant difference between the number of errors in the first and second drafts of their papers. The only thing that typically improves across drafts is legibility of handwriting. Although this is an important accomplishment for some students, making their text more readable, it does not improve the content of their message.

Writing is typically produced with an intended audience in mind. For example, it is not unusual for a teacher to ask children to write a story to share with their peers. Unfortunately, struggling writers pay little attention to their intended audience when revising. When we asked students with learning disabilities ages 10–12 to identify sentences in their papers that were in need of revision and then select an evaluation statement that best captured the problem, only 6% of their evaluations focused on the possible reaction of the reader (Graham, 1997). This primarily involved the concern that the reader would not understand some part of the sentence. Weaker writers often have difficulty taking the perspective of an absent reader (Flower, 1979; Sperling, 1996).

KNOWLEDGE OF WRITING

While reading another one of Snoopy's papers, Lucy complains that Snoopy's stories are pointless and his writing is bad. Snoopy is not worried, however, because his margins are neat. Clearly, Snoopy's understanding of what constitutes good writing needs work.

Students with learning disabilities also place too much emphasis on rules of usage, spelling, handwriting, and so forth. When we asked a child with a learning disability to describe good writing, she responded, "Spell every word right." A second child recommended, "Write as neat as you can." A third child advised, "Put your date and name on there . . . be sure to hold your pencil right." Children with learning disabilities are much more likely to stress form or mechanics, rather than substance or process, when defining good writing (Graham, Schwartz, & MacArthur, 1993; Wong, Wong, & Blenkinsop, 1989), possibly because much of their writing instruction focuses on the former and not the latter. This emphasis on form is further evident in their revising behavior, in which they concentrate most of their efforts on repairing mechanical miscues and making text neater (MacArthur & Graham, 1987; MacArthur, Graham, & Schwartz, 1991).

These children's knowledge about writing—its genres, devices, and conventions—is also quite limited. Even with a relatively familiar genre like story writing, students with learning disabilities may be unable to identify basic attributes or elements. For example, when we asked a young man with a learning disability to tell his friend what kinds of things are included in a story, he started off on the right track, indicating, "I would tell him main character," but he quickly veered into questionable territory with "A subject, predicate, and main idea." In contrast, a child who was a better writer indicated that in a story, "There is a setting and characters. There is some problem and they [characters] try to solve it. They do different things and something works and that is the end. And oh, yeah, you learn something, like a lesson." For students with learning disabilities, their incomplete knowledge is reflected in the stories they write, as they often omit basic story elements such as location, problem, ending, or moral (Graham & Harris, 1989a).

Self-Efficacy

After checking the mailbox, Charlie Brown gives Snoopy several humiliating rejection slips. The first insults his writing, and the second threatens violence to his mailbox if he tries to submit another story. Charlie Brown adds these letters to a closet already full of rejection slips. As always, however, Snoopy's confidence remains high.

Students with learning disabilities also appear to be more confident than is warranted. When we assessed the self-efficacy of children with learning disabilities ages 10–14, they were just as confident about their writing capabilities as the good writers in their classroom (Graham et al., 1993). Both groups of students were positive about their abilities to get and organize ideas for writing, transcribe ideas into sentences, sustain their writing effort, and correct mistakes in their paper. They favorably rated their ability to write reports, stories, and book reports. These children reminded us of another student who declared, "I am the best they is in English."

There are several possible reasons why students with learning disabilities overestimate their writing capabilities. They may not have developed the skills needed to accurately assess their capabilities, or they may project a false sense of confidence to cover their embarrassment about their difficulties with writing (Alvarez & Adelman, 1986; Graham, Harris, & Mason, 2004). Although an unrealistically high estimate of ability may protect these students' self-esteem (Sawyer, Graham, & Harris, 1992), there is a downside. Children who overestimate their capabilities may fail to allocate needed resources and persistence because they believe that good writers, like themselves, don't need to plan or exert much effort to write well.

Transcription Skills

Sitting at a desk at Charlie Brown's school, Snoopy is trying to remember the *I before E except after C* rule. He gets it all confused, however, making it *3 before 2 except after 10*.

Students with learning disabilities experience similar difficulties mastering the skills for transcribing oral language into written language. They routinely misspell words and ignore or misplace capitalization and punctuation (Graham et al., 1991). Many produce letters slowly, trudging along at almost half the rate of their more fluent peers (Weintraub & Graham, 1998). These difficulties not only make papers more difficult to read but can undermine the writing process in at least three ways (Graham, 1999; Scardamalia, Bereiter, & Goleman, 1982). First, possible writing content may be lost because writing is not fast enough to keep up with the child's thoughts. Second, having to switch attention to mechanical concerns, such as how to spell a word correctly, may disrupt other writing processes like planning upcoming text. Third, it may be more difficult to make text precisely fit intentions if the child's attention is occupied with mechanical concerns.

For the most part, the writing strategies presented in this book do not address the transcription difficulties faced by students with learning disabilities. The only exception is several revising strategies that include editing procedures for spelling, capitalization, punctuation, and other transcription difficulties. Because transcription problems can impede other composing processes, an effective writing program involves more than just teaching writing strategies. It also includes helping students master the skills needed for transcribing oral language into written language.

An Example and a Solution

Children should be required to clean their room, because they might think its ok to make messes at school. They may not find school work to turn in. They might lose important books. They might break important stuff like school books, projects, library books, and toys. In conclusion, it's just better to have a clean room.

Ron, a bright 12-year-old boy with a learning disability, wrote this short essay about whether children should be required to clean their own rooms (Graham & Harris, 1999). He would definitely agree with the observation by the novelist Gustave Flaubert that "writing is a dog's life," but Ron would disagree with the rest of Flaubert's commentary that it is "the only life worth living." Ron avoids writing whenever possible and devotes little effort to composing when asked to write. Despite his obvious dislike for writing, he is generally positive about his writing capabilities, telling others, "I'm pretty good at this."

Before starting the essay above, Ron complained, "Writing is stupid." His teacher ignored the comment and encouraged him to do his best writing, reminding him to "take your time and plan what you will say first." Ron ignored her advice and immediately started to write. He wrote quickly, taking short pauses to think about the spelling of a word or to consider what to say next. He did not evaluate the plausibility of the reasons used to support his premise, that children should be required to clean their room. His first reason—"they might think its ok to make messes at school"—is not very convincing. One of the two subsequent reasons—"they might break important stuff"—is weakened by the types of examples provided: school books and library books. All told, Ron spent 5 minutes writing this paper. When he wrote the last word, he quickly put it in his writing folder without reading it or making any corrections. Because he did not have effective strategies for planning, evaluating, and revising his writing, Ron applied a least-effort approach to composing, getting the task done as quickly as possible.

During a writing conference the next day, the teacher suggested that Ron make his argument stronger by including additional reasons and details. When he revised the paper, however, he spent most of his time trying to correct spelling miscues and rewriting the essay to make it look neater. Ron did make a few word changes and added another example to "stuff" that might get broken (i.e., "my little league baseball trophies"), but he added no new supporting reasons to his composition. While revising, he twice said aloud, "I hate this." He was frustrated because he did not have the know-how to make his paper better.

An important goal in writing instruction for students like Ron, who find writing challenging, is to help them change their approach to composing. This includes teaching them writing strategies for planning, setting goals, gathering and organizing information, monitoring and evaluating, revising, sustaining the writing effort, and orchestrating the writing process. These are the same types of tools used by more skilled writers (Graham & Harris, 2003a, 2003b; Hayes & Flower, 1986; Scardamalia & Bereiter, 1986). Learning how to use these tools improves writing performance, increases writing knowledge, enhances motivation, and sharpens self-efficacy (Graham & Harris, 1993). In the next three sections of this book, we examine a variety of writing strategies that are effective for students with learning disabilities.

Strategies for Teaching Planning, Writing, and Revising

"There is no royal road to learning."

This English proverb captures a fundamental truth about learning: Some things cannot be learned quickly and easily. They require both time and effort. This is also the case for learning the planning, writing, and revising strategies presented in this book. It is not enough to devote a single day to their mastery, as we have seen some teachers do. Rather, instruction must be carefully crafted and substantial enough so that students not only gain control over their use of the strategy but come to value it as well. In this section, we present a model for teaching writing strategies to students with learning disabilities. This model is designed to help students learn to apply the planning, writing, and revising strategies presented in Chapters 4–14 independently, effectively, and thoughtfully.

CHAPTER 3

How to Teach Writing Strategies

*"I hear and I forget.
I see and I remember. I do and I understand."*

This ancient Chinese proverb speaks directly to teaching writing strategies. Describing a strategy, how to use it, and why it is effective is essential, but this is only the start. Students need to see how the strategy works and practice using it themselves.

To be effective with students with learning disabilities, strategy instruction must also address these children's unique learning needs. Unfortunately, instruction in many classrooms follows a one-size-fits-all approach (see Graham, Harris, MacArthur, Chorzempa-Fink, 2003, for an example). The late comedian Milton Berle recognized this when he responded to "Son, I'm worried about you being at the bottom of the class" with "Pop, they teach the same stuff at both ends."

Students with learning disabilities typically require more intense and explicit instruction to master strategies that other children acquire more easily (Reeve & Brown, 1985; Wong, 1994). As a result, it is usually necessary to

- Supply additional explanations about the strategy, its parts, and how it works
- Teach prerequisite skills and processes needed to use the strategy effectively
- Remodel how to apply the strategy
- Develop mnemonic devices and charts to help students remember the steps of the strategy
- Provide extended feedback and support as students practice using the strategy

- Make instruction based on criteria rather than time

- Teach students procedures to help them better regulate their use of the strategy

- Address roadblocks that interfere with learning the strategy

Such procedures help guarantee that students with learning disabilities acquire the skills needed to apply writing strategies correctly, but this is still not enough. Strategic behavior involves will as well as skill. As an ancient Chinese proverb notes, "Teachers open the door, but you must enter yourself."

The importance of will or motivation cannot be underestimated. Using a new strategy or approach to solve a problem requires both intention and effort. In the case of writing, students with learning disabilities must set aside their typical knowledge-telling approach to composing and purposefully apply the new strategy. This is not as easy as it sounds. First, their old strategy may be successful in some instances. For example, knowledge-telling or writing-as-remembering works quite well for some types of writing assignments, such as composing a personal narrative. Because knowledge-telling works some of the time (reinforcing students' use of it) and requires little effort, children may not readily apply a new and more demanding strategy (Ellis, 1986). Second, students may not use a new strategy because they do not value it (Salomon & Globerson, 1987). This may occur because they do not believe that the strategy is effective or they have had little voice or investment in learning it. Thus, effective instruction promotes students' will to use a new strategy through

- Enthusiastic teaching

- Establishing the importance of effort in learning and using the strategy

- Promoting an "I can do" attitude

- Providing opportunities for students to establish how the strategy improves their writing

- Praising and reinforcing students' effort and use of the strategy

- Including students as active collaborators in the learning process

- Fostering students' ownership of the strategy

Finally, the application of a new strategy is not just dependent on mastering how to do it and being motivated to use it; it requires knowing when and where to apply it and how to adapt it to new situations (Salomon & Perkins, 1989). This is especially important for students with learning disabilities, as they are less likely than their peers with typical achievement to apply available strategies to new situations (Wong, 1994). Consequently, strategy instruction for these students must include procedures that promote both maintenance and generalization of strategy use.

In this chapter, we present a model of strategy instruction that includes procedures for addressing each of these issues. This approach, *self-regulated strategy development* (SRSD) instruction (Harris & Graham, 1996) has been used to teach many of the writing strategies presented in this book. To date, 25 studies have examined the effectiveness of using SRSD to teach strategies in writing, with the majority of these studies involving students with learning disabilities (see Graham & Harris, 2003a). These studies included the teaching of a variety of planning, writing, and revising strategies for both narrative and expository text. This approach to strategy instruction is very successful with students with and without learning disabilities. For example, the average effect size for improvement in writing quality for students with learning disabilities receiving SRSD instruction in these studies was 1.14. (An effect size is calculated by subtracting the posttest mean of the control group from the SRSD group and dividing that number by the standard deviation of the control group. An effect size greater than .80 is considered large.)

We first provide an overview of the SRSD model and then present three examples illustrating how to apply this approach. The first example involves a special and a general educator teaching the *story grammar strategy* (presented in Chapter 10) in an inclusive fifth-grade classroom. The second example focuses on teaching the *three-step strategy with TREE* (see Chapter 11) to a small group of fifth- and sixth-grade students with learning disabilities. The third example involves one-to-one instruction with the *STOP and LIST strategy* (see Chapter 6) with fifth-grade students with learning disabilities. The SRSD teaching procedures differ slightly in each of these examples, as teachers placed greater emphasis on certain aspects of the model to make it fit their students and situation.

THE SELF-REGULATED STRATEGY DEVELOPMENT MODEL

With SRSD, students are explicitly taught planning or revising strategies in combination with procedures for regulating the use of these strategies, the writing task, and any undesirable behaviors (e.g., impulsivity) that may impede their performance (Harris & Graham, 1996, 1999). This model of instruction is designed to enhance students' strategic behaviors, self-regulation skills, content knowledge, and motivational dispositions. SRSD is responsive to the needs of students with learning disabilities because the students often have difficulty in each of these areas (Harris, Graham, & Deshler, 1998). They typically use inefficient and ineffective strategies, experience difficulty activating and regulating strategic behavior, possess incomplete and poorly integrated knowledge, hold maladaptive beliefs and self-doubts, and exhibit low levels of engagement (Ellis, 1986; Graham & Harris, 2003a; Wong, 1994).

SRSD elevates strategic knowledge by teaching students more sophisticated strategies for accomplishing writing tasks. Self-regulation is advanced by teaching students how to use goal setting, self-monitoring, self-instruction, and/or self-reinforcement to manage their use of the target strategies, the writing task, and their behaviors. (Self-monitoring and goal setting are also examined in Chapters 15 and 16.) Content knowledge is increased by teaching any information or skills students need in order to use the selected strategies or self-regulation procedures. Motivation is boosted by a variety of procedures, including emphasizing the role of effort in learning, making concrete and visible the positive effects of instruction, and emphasizing the student's role as an active collaborator in the learning process.

Six instructional stages provide the structural framework for SRSD. These stages provide a set of general guidelines for instruction, but stages can be reordered, combined, or modified to meet student and teacher needs.

Develop Background Knowledge

Students are taught the knowledge and skills needed to understand, acquire, and execute the writing strategy and self-regulation procedures.

Discuss It   The teacher and students examine and discuss current writing performance and the strategies used to accomplish specific writing tasks. The target strategy, its purpose and benefits, and how and when to use it are examined. Students are then asked to make a commitment to learn the strategy and act as a collaborative partner in this endeavor. Negative or interfering self-talk or beliefs that students currently use may also be addressed at this time. The concept of *progress monitoring*, or teaching students how to monitor the impact of learning the strategy, may be presented as well.

Model It   The teacher models aloud how to use the strategy, employing appropriate self-talk and self-instructions. Self-instructions include a combination of problem definition, planning, strategy use, self-evaluation, error correction, coping, and self-reinforcement statements. After analyzing the teacher's performance, the teacher and students may collaborate on how to change the strategy to make it more effective or efficient. Each student develops and records personal self-statements he or she plans to use. These self-statements may be designed to regulate strategy use, the writing task, or interfering student behavior. Teachers may model how to use the strategy more than once, depending upon how quickly students grasp the illustrated concepts. The concept of *goal setting*, or teaching students to set performance goals for improving their writing through the use of the strategy, may occur during this stage as well.

Memorize It   The steps of the strategy, any accompanying mnemonic for remembering them, and students' personalized self-statements are memorized; paraphrasing is allowed as long as the original meaning is maintained. Practice memorizing the strategies, mnemonics, and personalized self-statements may actually start during the Discuss It stage and continue into the next stage, Support It.

Support It   Students practice using the writing strategy, self-statements, and any other self-regulation processes (e.g., progress monitoring and goal setting) already introduced, receiving help from the teacher, their peers, or both until they can use these procedures independently. Teacher help ranges from direct assistance in applying the strategy, to remodeling, to corrective feedback and praise. Students may also support each other by working together as they initially learn to apply the strategies. Both teacher and peer help, as well as instructional aids such as self-statement lists and strategy reminder charts, are faded as soon as possible, and students are encouraged to begin using personal self-statements privately (i.e., in their minds).

Independent Performance   Students use the writing strategy independently. If goal setting and progress-monitoring procedures are still in use, the teacher may decide to fade them at this time.

Procedures for promoting maintenance and generalization are integrated throughout the six stages. These include

- Identifying opportunities to use the writing strategy outside of the training situation

- Examining how to modify the writing strategy for the situations identified

- Setting goals to use the strategy with new tasks

- Discussing the results of using the strategy with these tasks

- Asking teachers, peers, or both to prompt strategy use

- Encouraging teachers to comment on exactly how the strategy improved the students' writing

FOUR CRITICAL CHARACTERISTICS

In addition to the six stages of instruction, there are four critical characteristics of SRSD instruction. First, teachers are enthusiastic about the effects of learning the strategy and are positive about their students' capabilities. Second, children are viewed as active collaborators who work with the teacher and each other during instruction. Third, instruction is individualized so that each student receives the support needed to master the strategy and accompanying self-regulation procedures. Fourth, instruction is based on criteria rather than time; students move through each instructional process at their own pace and do not proceed to later stages of instruction until they have met the criteria for doing so.

Example 1: Teaching the Story Grammar Strategy

Our first example focuses on teaching the story grammar strategy to a class of fifth-grade students that included three children with learning disabilities (Danoff et al., 1993). This strategy for planning and writing a story involves generating ideas for each basic part of a story in advance of writing. This initial plan is then embellished and upgraded as students write. The steps of the strategy are presented in Figure 3.1.

The students in the participating class attended an inclusive school. Their writing class was team taught by a special education teacher, Barbara, and a general education teacher, Joan. After reviewing students' writing portfolios, Barbara and Joan decided to teach the story grammar strategy to the whole class. Some of the students in the class, including those with learning disabilities, wrote stories that were incomplete. The two teachers also noted that the story writing of all of the other students in the class could be improved by including greater detail and elaboration as well as more action. Barbara and Joan further wanted to help several students who were anxious about writing establish a stronger sense of motivation and an "I can do this if I try" attitude. This included all of the students with learning disabilities and several other struggling writers.

Step 1. Think of a story that you would like to share with others.

Step 2. Let your mind be free.

Step 3. Write down the story part reminder:
   W - W - W
   WHAT = 2
   HOW = 2

   Make notes for each question below:
   Who is the main character; who else is in the story?
   When does the story take place?
   Where does the story take place?
   What does the main character want to do; what do the other characters want to do?
   What happens when the main character tries to do it; what happens with the other characters?
   How does the story end?
   How does the main character feel; how do other characters feel?

Step 4. Make notes of your ideas for each part.

Step 5. Write your story—use good parts, add, elaborate, or revise as you write or afterward, and make sense.

Writing Better: Effective Strategies for Teaching Students with Learning Difficulties, by S. Graham and K.R. Harris, © 2005 Paul H. Brookes Publishing Co., Inc. All rights reserved.
Figure 3.1.   Story grammar strategy.

It was decided that Barbara, the special education teacher, would take the lead in teaching the strategy, but both teachers would play an active role, allowing them to better individualize instruction. Instruction in the strategy occurred during Writers' Workshop (Atwell, 1987; Graves, 1983). With this approach, a routine is established in which students plan, write a first draft of, revise, edit, and publish their paper. As they are working on their composition, students hold regular conferences with teachers about the work, share in-progress and completed work with classmates, select papers for publication, and reflect on their writing accomplishments and challenges in a journal. In Barbara and Joan's classroom, students were also encouraged to consult with a peer when planning and revising their papers. Although students typically choose the topics for their papers in Writers' Workshop, Barbara and Joan decided that the students' writing would focus on composing stories. The first stages of strategy instruction were offered as an extended series of mini-lessons, lasting approximately 30 minutes each. Once students moved to the Support It stage, they practiced using the strategy as part of the regular Workshop approach.

SRSD Instruction   Instruction began with a conference with the entire class (Develop Background Knowledge, Discuss It). The class discussed what they knew about story writing, including what parts are commonly found in a story (i.e., setting, characters' goals, actions to achieve the goals, ending, and characters' reactions). The story grammar strategy was briefly described, and the class talked about how including and expanding story parts can improve a story. Barbara and Joan established the goals for learning the strategy (to write better stories, ones that are more fun to write and more fun for others to read). They also described the procedures for learning the strategy, emphasizing students' roles as collaborators (including the possibility of serving as a peer tutor for other students learning the strategy in the future) and the importance of effort in mastering the strategy. Each student was asked to make a commitment to learn the strategy, and each one did.

During the next mini-lesson, the class resumed the previous discussion on story parts, focusing on setting (characters, place, and time) and story episode (precipitating event, characters' goals, action to achieve goals, resolution, and characters' reactions). The students located examples of these elements in books they had read, highlighting the different ways authors used and developed the story parts. To promote linkages to reading, the class also considered how knowledge of story parts can help the reader understand the author's message. To ensure that students understood each story element, the teacher asked them to generate ideas for story parts using different story lines.

At this point, students selected at least one or two previously written stories from their portfolios and determined which parts were present in each story. Barbara and Joan showed students how to graph the number of parts included in their story. They then explained that students keep a graph showing the number of parts in each story written as they learned to use the strategy. This self-regulation procedure allows the students to monitor the completeness of their stories and the effects of learning the strategy. Barbara and Joan checked with each student to see that he or she correctly graphed the story parts, and they provided additional assistance later to any student experiencing difficulty. For students who included all or nearly all story parts in previously written stories, the two teachers stressed that more detail, elaboration, and action could improve their parts.

In the third mini-lesson, Barbara reintroduced the story grammar strategy. Each student had a chart listing the strategy steps and a mnemonic (WWW, What = 2, How = 2) for remembering the questions for the parts of a story (see Step 3 in Figure 3.1). Barbara asked students what they thought the reason might be for each step. They then discussed where and how to use the strategy. Students indicated that the strategy could be used to write stories, book reports, and biographies. They also indicated that paying attention to story parts could help them with reading.

During the next lesson (which lasted a full hour), Barbara shared one of her ideas for a story with the class and then modeled (while thinking out loud) how to use the story writing strategy to develop this idea (Model It). Students participated in this activity by helping her as she planned and made notes for each story part and as she wrote the first draft. (Changes to her plan were made several times as she wrote.) Before planning the story, Barbara set a goal to include all story parts and "think of a lot of ideas for each one." She then explained that students were expected to set a similar goal before writing their stories and to check to see if they met it once they were finished.

While she planned and wrote her story, Barbara used a variety of self-statements to direct the use of the strategy, her behavior, and the writing process. This included statements involving problem definition ("What do I need to do?"), planning ("First, I need to think of ideas for my story"), self-evaluation ("Does this part make sense?"), self-reinforcement ("What a great ending"), and coping ("I can do this"). She also used self-statements designed to help her with the process of brainstorming ideas. These included self-instructions such as "Let my mind be free" and "Take my time; good ideas will come to me."

Once the story was completed, Barbara and the class looked to see whether all of the parts were included in the story and whether each part was fully presented. She verbally reinforced herself for achieving her goal and graphed the results, commenting that "I got them all because of my hard work and use of the strategy."

The class then discussed the importance of what people say to themselves as they work and write. Students volunteered examples of positive and sometimes negative things they said when writing. The class then identified the types of things Barbara said that helped her use the strategy and do a good job of writing the story. Next, students developed (and recorded on a card) personal self-statements they planned to use while writing. Examples of students' personalized self-statements included

- "How am I doing so far?"
- "I can do this if I try."
- "Slow down and take my time."

At this time, Barbara and Joan asked the students to suggest any changes they thought would make the strategy better. No changes were suggested, so the two teachers revisited this issue in later lessons.

In the next mini-lesson, students were asked to memorize the mnemonic, the strategy steps, and the self-statements they planned to use (Memorize It). Barbara and Joan explained that it would be easier to use the strategy if students were not always having to look up the steps, mnemonic, and so forth. Students practiced memorizing these items alone or with a partner. Most of the students memorized these items easily, while others continued to practice as the class moved to the next stage of instruction, Support It.

Students began to use the writing strategy and self-regulation procedures to write their own stories during Writers' Workshop, receiving assistance from Barbara and Joan as needed (Support It). For the students with learning disabilities and for a few other struggling writers, this stage began by collaboratively planning a story with Barbara. This allowed the teacher to make sure that these students correctly understood how to use the strategy steps, the mnemonic, and self-regulation procedures (goal setting, self-statements, and counting and graphing story parts). The other students in the classroom began this stage by collaboratively writing a story with a peer. Joan provided them with help as needed.

As students practiced applying the strategy during Writers' Workshop, Barbara and Joan modified the amount and intensity of their support. Assistance included helping students determine self-statements that were especially useful to them, as well as reinforcing explanation and modeling of the strategy or self-regulation procedures. In some instances, assistance focused on planning for greater detail and elaboration or increasing the goals and actions of the characters in the story. Support, including students' use of the strategy chart and list of personalized self-statements, was faded as soon as possible. This included encouraging students to use their self-statements in their minds if they were not already doing so.

Most students were able to apply the story grammar strategy and accompanying self-regulation procedures correctly and efficiently after writing three stories. Students who continued to need assistance received it from Barbara and Joan until they could use the strategy easily and independently (Independent Performance). Students were told that they were no longer required to set goals or count and graph story parts, but they were encouraged to do so because it would help ensure that they wrote complete and interesting stories.

A class conference was held at this point to evaluate the strategy. Students told Barbara and Joan that the strategy helped them write better stories and that they were glad that they had learned how to use it. The mnemonic was most frequently nominated as the best part of the strategy. The students also identified opportunities in which they could apply what they had learned, and they agreed to hold a review session once per month to revisit how to apply the strategy, as well as their successes in using it.

Example 2: Teaching the Three-Step Strategy with TREE

Our second example involves teaching the three-step strategy with TREE to a small group of fifth- and sixth-grade students with learning disabilities (Sexton, Harris, & Graham, 1998). This strategy for planning and writing a persuasive essay includes a series of steps designed to help writers identify what they plan to accomplish, generate an initial content outline, and continue to expand and modify that outline while writing. The steps of the strategy are presented in Figure 3.2.

As in the previous example, the participating students attended an inclusive school. Their multigrade writing class was team taught by a special education teacher, Marva, and a general education teacher, John. The students continued to participate in Writers' Workshop (Atwell, 1987), the classroom writing program, while receiving small-group SRSD instruction with Marva. Students were used to working in small groups with either Marva or John because students in this multigrade class were frequently regrouped for different periods or subjects.

These students were selected to receive SRSD instruction because each had difficulty with writing, displayed a low level of motivation, and had maladaptive beliefs about the causes of writing success and failure. Marva and John also wanted them to improve

---

Step 1. Who will read my paper?
          Why am I writing this paper?

Step 2. Plan what to say using **TREE**
          Note **T**opic Sentence
          Note **R**easons
          Examine Each Reason—Will My Reader Buy It?
          Note **E**nding

Step 3. Write and say more.

Writing Better: Effective Strategies for Teaching Students with Learning Difficulties, by S. Graham and K.R. Harris,
Figure 3.2.   The three-step strategy with TREE.

their persuasive essay-writing skills, as they perceived these to be important not only for upper elementary school, but for the coming middle and high school years as well.

SRSD Instruction   Marva began instruction by leading a discussion on what students already knew about persuasive essays, including identifying the parts or elements that are commonly found in such a paper (Develop Background Knowledge). This knowledge is an essential prerequisite to using the three-step strategy with TREE because these elements serve as prompts for generating possible writing content (see Step 2, Figure 3.3). Marva and her students discussed three types of common persuasive essay elements: premise, supporting reasons, and conclusion. They then identified examples of these elements in persuasive essays they were reading in class and essays written by other children. Next, they generated ideas for each essay part, using different topics.

Following this initial lesson, Marva held a conference with each student (Discuss It). She and each student talked about strategies that the student currently used when writing. At this time, Marva indicated that she was planning to teach the students a strategy for writing persuasive essays. They talked about the goals for learning the strategy (to write better essays and develop a strong opinion) and how including and expanding essay parts could improve writing. Marva also introduced the concept of progress monitoring, indicating that self-assessment would allow the student to monitor the completeness of persuasive essays written during instruction and to assess the impact of using the strategy. Together, they counted and graphed the number of elements included in a previously written essay. Marva explained to the student that the number of elements in each essay would be counted and graphed during instruction. Before completing the conference, Marva emphasized the student's role as a collaborator, and they conjointly developed a written goal to learn the strategy.

After the individual conferences, Marva and her students resumed their small-group discussion of the writing strategy. Each student had a chart listing the steps of the strategy (see Figure 3.3). Marva asked students what they thought the reason for each step might be. The group then discussed how and when to use the strategy (e.g., whenever you are asked to tell what you believe or give your opinion). Marva further described the procedures for learning the strategy, stressing the importance of effort, because a strategy can't work if students don't work hard to master it.

During the third lesson, Marva modeled how to use the three-step strategy with TREE, while thinking out loud (Model It). The students helped her as she planned and

---

Step 1. STOP: **S**top and **T**hink **O**f **P**urposes.

                    and

Step 2. LIST: **L**ist **I**deas and **S**equence **T**hem.

Step 3. Write and say more.

Writing Better: Effective Strategies for Teaching Students with Learning Difficulties, by S. Graham and K.R. Harris, © 2005 Paul H. Brookes Publishing Co., Inc. All rights reserved.
Figure 3.3.   Steps of the STOP and LIST strategy.

wrote the first draft. Working together, they accepted and rejected possible ideas to support Marva's premise and continued to modify the plan while writing their paper. Once the first draft was completed, Marva and her students reread the paper and made revisions.

As she modeled the strategy, Marva used a variety of self-statements to help her manage the strategy, the writing process, and her behavior. These included problem definition (e.g., "What do I need to do?"), planning (e.g., "Okay, first I need to . . ."), self-evaluation (e.g., "Did I say what I really believe?"), and self-reinforcement statements (e.g., "Great, this is a good reason"). She frequently attributed her success in writing the persuasive essay to effort and use of the strategy. Examples of these attributional self-statements included "If I work hard and follow the steps of the strategy, I'll write a good essay" and "I want to write a good essay, so I will try hard to use the strategy and include good essay parts."

After modeling how to use the strategy, Marva and her students discussed the importance of what people say to themselves while they work. Students volunteered examples of personal positive and sometimes negative self-statements they used when writing. They also identified the things Marva said that helped her as she worked, stressing statements that emphasized the role of effort and strategy use. After discussing how these self-statements were helpful, each student generated and recorded on a small chart the self-statements he or she planned to use. This included developing at least one self-statement attributing success to effort or use of the strategy (e.g., "Work hard—Write better").

Students then worked on memorizing the steps of the strategy, the mnemonic (TREE), and several self-statements they planned to use during a fourth lesson (Memorize It). Each student practiced memorizing this information with another student. Partners typically practiced by quizzing each other. These items were memorized easily by most students, but some needed extended practice.

In subsequent lessons, students received help from Marva as they practiced using the writing strategy, self-statements, and progress-monitoring procedures to write opinion essays (Support It). Marva's goal during this stage of instruction was to support children's efforts as they were learning to use these procedures. She adjusted and modified her support as needed, reducing assistance as each child became increasingly adept at using the procedures.

At first, students received considerable support in developing a writing outline (Step 2 of the strategy). Based on her previous experience with the students, Marva thought that this part of the strategy would be most challenging for them. Support initially involved Marva acting as the lead collaborator during planning. As they planned together, Marva intentionally committed a few errors, such as forgetting a strategy step. This led to discussions about the impact and cause of such errors. Marva then modeled how to correct the mistake, combining the correction with a positive attributional statement, such as "I need to try to follow all of the strategy steps, so I can write a good essay." If students later made mistakes using the strategy, the possible consequences of the mistake were examined, and students were encouraged to redo the step while using a positive attributional statement.

Marva's role as a planning collaborator was soon replaced with less intrusive forms of assistance, such as a reminder to carry out a step, a prompt to devote more attention to a specific process (e.g., generate more possible supporting reasons), and feedback on the use of the strategy and accompanying self-regulation procedures. In some instances, it was necessary for Marva and a student to revisit the rationale underlying an individual step. Assistance also included helping students to determine which self-statements were most useful to them. Students' reliance on the strategy chart or self-statement lists as a reminder was faded, and Marva encouraged students to use their self-statements in their minds.

As students worked on their papers, Marva encouraged them to use goal setting and progress monitoring (counting and graphing elements) in conjunction with the writing strategy. Prior to planning an essay, students set a goal to include all of the parts of TREE in their papers. Once an essay was completed, students reviewed their papers, determining whether any parts were missing as well as counting and graphing the number of essay elements included. Students then shared their papers with each other, providing feedback on the strengths and weaknesses of each other's arguments.

After writing three or four essays, each student was able to use the writing strategy and self-regulation procedures without Marva's help. At this point, students planned and wrote essays independently (Independent Performance). Marva provided positive and constructive feedback as needed, and students continued to share their papers with each other. Students were asked to continue using goal setting and progress monitoring on at least two more essays. After that, they were not required to use these procedures, but they were encouraged to do so.

As a group, students discussed how the strategy they were learning could be used in other classes. Several students indicated that they now told themselves "to try harder" when writing or asked themselves if their paper "was good enough." Students identified opportunities for future use of the writing strategy and self-regulation procedures, and they discussed how they would need to adapt what they had learned. Each student also evaluated the strategy and the instructional process. When asked if they would change anything about instruction, the only recommendation was to give homework assignments to use the strategy.

Example 3: Teaching STOP and LIST

Our final example involves teaching the STOP and LIST strategy to three fifth-grade students with learning disabilities who were experiencing difficulty with writing (Troia et al., 1999). With this strategy, students set goals for their papers, generate possible writing ideas, and sequence these ideas before writing. They continue to expand and modify this initial outline as they write. The steps of the strategy are presented in Figure 3.3.

In contrast to the other two examples, STOP and LIST was taught by Gary, who was tutoring each child individually after school. The methods used to teach the strategy also differed in three important ways. Instead of first describing the strategy and asking students to reflect on the rationale and value of each step (as is typically done during Discuss It), Gary modeled how to do several tasks (using goal setting, brainstorming, and organizing). Students were then asked to identify the essential features, rationale, and value of the processes Gary used. A mnemonic was introduced as a way to help students remember to carry out these processes not only when writing but also with other tasks that involved planning. A second difference centered around the use of homework to promote maintenance and generalization. For each homework assignment, students identified an opportunity to apply the strategy to other tasks at home or school, how the strategy would help them with the task, and what modifications were needed. After completing the homework assignment, Gary and the student discussed the effects of using the strategy and any problems encountered. The third difference involved the emphasis on self-regulation strategies. In the two previous examples, students developed personal self-statements, set goals, and used a specific procedure to monitor their progress. When teaching STOP and LIST, the primary self-regulatory procedure involves self-evaluation and reflection, wherein the student considers how and why the strategy facilitated performance.

SRSD Instruction   Gary began the instruction by reviewing what each child knew about stories (Develop Background Knowledge). He planned to teach students to use STOP and LIST while writing stories, and he believed the strategy would have greater impact if each child was knowledgeable about the attributes of this genre. The instructional activities for developing this knowledge were similar to those used in the first example with story grammar strategy and are not iterated here.

Following this initial lesson, each student participated in three sessions in which Gary modeled how to do specific tasks using goal setting, brainstorming, and organizing (the primary processes included in STOP and LIST). After the task was modeled, Gary helped the student identify the essential processes he used to complete the task (Model It and Discuss It). STOP and LIST was then introduced as a reminder to use these processes with writing and with other tasks that involved planning.

In the first session, Gary modeled, while thinking out loud, the use of the three target processes to read a chapter and write a story. In reading the chapter, he first set a goal ("find out how plants fit into the food chain"), listed or brainstormed what he already knew, and organized his ideas by topics. As he read, Gary modified his outline by adding, deleting, changing, and rearranging ideas and categories. When writing a story, he set a goal ("to write a good story to share with my creative writing class"), brainstormed ideas to include in the story, and sequenced the ideas he planned to use. While writing, Gary modified his outline—adding, changing, deleting, and rearranging ideas. He provided a rationale for each thing he did while doing both tasks, and he verbally reinforced himself on a job well done. When Gary generated ideas, organized them, or modified his plan, the student was encouraged to help.

After the two tasks were modeled, the student was asked to take some time and think about what Gary did. To help the child identify the essential features, rationale, and value of the three processes used to accomplish the tasks, Gary guided the student's thinking by asking a series of questions. Questions initially focused on what Gary did that was similar in both tasks and what was different. All of the students were able to identify goal setting, brainstorming, and organizing as similar. Gary then focused the questions more tightly by asking the student to think about why he used each of these processes and how they helped him. Subsequent questions focused on how Gary's approach to writing a story differed from the child's own approach. The student was also asked to evaluate the possible use and advantage of each of the three processes in his or her own writing.

Identical procedures were used in the next two sessions in which Gary modeled preparing a speech, planning a trip, and writing a story. The only difference was that the student was asked to think about what Gary did that was similar and different across sessions. At this point, Gary introduced a mnemonic to help the child remember to set goals, brainstorm, and sequence when writing and doing other tasks involving planning. A small chart was used to introduce the mnemonic, STOP and LIST: *S*top, *T*hink *O*f *P*urpose, and *L*ist *I*deas, *S*equence *T*hem.

On the following day, discussion of STOP and LIST resumed with the student considering how goal setting, brainstorming, and sequencing might be helpful. A list was generated of when, where, and why the student previously used each of the processes. Gary then invited the child to learn how to use STOP and LIST and described the procedures for learning it. He noted that the purpose for learning the strategy was to "write better stories and use it with other tasks." The student then generated what he or she would do to facilitate learning the strategy (e.g., "not give up," "work hard").

At the end of this lesson, the student briefly practiced memorizing the mnemonic and the sentence it represented (Memorize It). This continued in succeeding lessons until the student could repeat it quickly and correctly.

In the next stage of instruction, the student received help from Gary while practicing using the strategy to write stories (Support It). Gary collaboratively planned a story with each student and made sure that the strategy and mnemonic were used appropriately. The chart with the mnemonic was used to remind students to set goals, brainstorm, and sequence. As the student became more adept at applying the strategy, Gary modified the amount of help provided. Assistance typically included prompts, guidance and feedback, and re-explanations. This help, including the use of the mnemonic chart, was faded as quickly as possible for each child.

After writing a story, students identified why they were successful, unsuccessful, or both; assessed the role of goal setting, brainstorming, and sequencing in writing the story; and considered what else they could have done to write an even better story. Each student also identified an opportunity to apply STOP and LIST at home or school, indicating how it would be helpful and what modifications were needed to make it work. Examples of homework included planning a trip, writing a report, or getting ready for school. At the start of the next lesson, the student provided evidence that he or she had used the strategy to complete the homework assignment. The student and Gary also discussed how the strategy helped him or her carry out the task successfully. In addition, each child described any other times when goal setting, brainstorming, or sequencing had been used since the previous lesson. Examples generated by the children focused mainly on the completion of writing assignments.

After writing just two stories, each student was able to use STOP and LIST without instructor support. From that point on, students planned and wrote stories independently (Independent Performance). Gary provided positive and constructive feedback as needed, and students continued to use the strategy to complete homework assignments.

Gary discontinued instruction when a child could use the strategy independently to write a story and when two homework assignments in a row were completed successfully. Once this goal was met, the student was asked to reconsider how the processes of goal setting, brainstorming, and sequencing were helpful when writing stories and completing homework assignments. Gary and the student further discussed how STOP and LIST had to be modified for these tasks, and they identified opportunities for applying the strategy in the future (e.g., writing assignments, doing homework, shopping, organizing a room).

A FINAL OBSERVATION

The famed Italian educator Maria Montessori observed that success occurs when a teacher is able to say, "The children are now working as if I did not exist." This is the ultimate goal of strategy instruction in writing. As one teacher told us, "When students know how to do it, they light their own way."

Writing Strategies that Can Be Applied Broadly

Skilled writers possess a mental tool kit containing strategies for creating text, gathering information, organizing ideas, revising, and so forth. John Steinbeck, the author of *The Grapes of Wrath*, fleshed out his thoughts by visualizing them so clearly that he could even see the color of different objects in his visions. Henry David Thoreau never missed an opportunity to capture a possible idea, sleeping with a pen on the nightstand and a piece of paper under his pillow. Leo Tolstoy, the author of *Anna Karenina*, reorganized his writing from the previous day by attacking it with scissors and paste, cutting and rearranging it as needed.

These strategies all have one thing in common. They can be applied broadly to a variety of different writing genres. In this section, we examine six validated strategies for planning and revising that can be used with both narrative and expository text. With the first strategy, *PLEASE*, students learn how to write paragraphs that contain a topic sentence, supporting details, and a concluding statement (Chapter 4). The second strategy, *PLANS*, breaks down the writing process into the following three steps: develop a plan for what the paper will accomplish, apply the plan flexibly while writing the paper, and revise the paper if any part of the plan is not completed as intended (Chapter 5). With the third strategy, *STOP and LIST*, students plan their papers by setting writing goals, generating possible writing content, and sequencing the ideas they plan to use (Chapter 6). A fourth strategy, *peer revising*, involves students working together to improve both the substance and form of their papers (Chapter 7). The fifth strategy, *CDO*, structures the revising process so that the separate elements of revising are coordinated and occur in a regular way and at the right time (Chapter 8). With the final strategy, *summary writing*, students summarize in writing the material they have read (Chapter 9).

The format for presenting each strategy includes describing the strategy, examining how to teach it, providing the scientific evidence on its effectiveness with students with learning disabilities, specifying other groups of students that might profit from learning it, and considering how it can be extended and modified.

When presenting the scientific evidence on the effectiveness of a strategy, we first describe the children who were taught to use it and then present information on its impact. For single-subject design studies, this includes information on students' percentage of improvement (e.g., quality scores rose 175% following instruction). For large-group studies, it involves the presentation of effect sizes. Effect sizes are computed by subtracting the posttest mean of the control group from the posttest mean of the treatment group and dividing by the standard deviation for the control group. An effect size of .20 is considered small, .50 is medium, and .80 is large. Whenever possible, we provide sample compositions that illustrate the impact of the strategy on students' writing.

Three of the strategies included in this section are taught using the *self-regulated strategy development* (SRSD) model (see Chapter 3). For the sake of brevity, we do not repeatedly present this model when describing how to teach these three strategies (i.e., PLANS, STOP and LIST, and peer revising). Instead, we refer the reader to Chapter 3, where a full description of SRSD and examples of how to implement it are provided. Instructional issues that are specific to each strategy, however, are addressed here. Finally, the teaching methods for the other three strategies (PLEASE, CDO, and summary writing) are fully described in their corresponding chapters.

CHAPTER 4

PLEASE

A Paragraph-Writing Strategy

Robert Hendrickson, author of *The Literary Life and Other Curiosities*, indicated that his best rule for writing paragraphs was based on the legendary practice of typesetters: "Set type as long as you can hold your breath without getting blue in the face, then put in a comma; when you yawn put in a semicolon; and when you want to sneeze, that's time for a paragraph."

It sometimes seems that students with learning disabilities and other struggling writers follow this same recipe and not the more accepted maxim that a paragraph is a group of related ideas about the same thing. If they form paragraphs at all, students with learning disabilities too often jumble relevant and irrelevant ideas together. This is evident in the following paragraph about George Washington:

> George Washington is one of my favorites like when he didn't let the British know he was out of bulits and kept firing. I read many things on him in a book. It was a brown one for 14 days. I am glad he comes but once a year.

The *PLEASE strategy* provides a more structured formula for writing one of the most common types of paragraphs, namely, one in which the main idea is stated (Welch, 1992). PLEASE also provides students with a road map for how to write cogent paragraphs—ones with appropriate details and clearly defined boundaries.

THE PLEASE STRATEGY FOR WRITING PARAGRAPHS

The PLEASE strategy provides a heuristic for writing a paragraph (Welch, 1992). PLEASE is a mnemonic that reminds students to carry out the following steps:

Step 1. Pick: The first step of the mnemonic reminds students to pick the topic, audience, and type of paragraph they plan to write. The types of paragraph include enumerative (i.e., ideas are listed), compare/contrast (i.e., similarities or differences described), and cause and effect (i.e., an event and its effect are described).

Step 2. List: The second step directs students to generate a list of ideas they might include in the paragraph. This includes listing any criteria that might be used to evaluate these ideas, such as believability.

Step 3. Evaluate: Students then evaluate their list to see if it is complete and contains all relevant ideas. Additional ideas are added as needed. If other evaluation criteria were specified during Step 2, they are also applied at this point. Once the evaluation is completed, students sequence or organize the ideas they plan to use.

Step 4. Activate: Next, students activate the paragraph by constructing a topic sentence. They are encouraged to generate a short declarative sentence that introduces the reader to the topic.

Step 5. Supply: Using their list of ideas, students supply or construct sentences that support the topic sentence. They are asked to turn each relevant idea into a sentence and supply examples and elaborations where appropriate.

Step 6. End: The final step is to end with a concluding sentence. This includes rephrasing the topic sentence by using synonyms to generate a statement that wraps up the paragraph. Students also "police" their paragraph to correct miscues in capitalization, overall appearance, punctuation, and spelling. To help them remember to revise these errors, they use the *COPS strategy* described by Ellis and Lenz (1987) (see Figure 4.1).

- Have I **C**apitalized the first word and proper nouns?
- How is the **O**verall appearance?
- Have I used end **P**unctuation, commas, and semicolons correctly?
- Do the words look like they are **S**pelled right? Can I sound them out, or should I use a dictionary?

Writing Better: Effective Strategies for Teaching Students with Learning Difficulties, by S. Graham and K.R. Harris, © 2005 Paul H. Brookes Publishing Co., Inc. All rights reserved.
Figure 4.1. The COPS strategy.

Teaching the Strategy

Welch (1992) provided little information on how to teach the PLEASE strategy. She did indicate that teachers taught the strategy three times per week during 30-minute lessons for approximately 20 weeks. Furthermore, teachers used an instructional manual to guide their activities and instructional videos that supported the teaching of the strategy. Because these materials are not readily available or described elsewhere, we recommend that teachers use the steps listed below to teach this strategy.

Step 1. Begin instruction by asking students to read several examples of well- and poorly written paragraphs. Discuss with students how well- and poorly written paragraphs differ. Emphasize the parts of a well-written paragraph (topic sentence, supporting details, and concluding sentence); how the information in a well-written paragraph fits together or is typically about one thing; and how writers mark the beginning of a paragraph by indenting or skipping a line. Discuss with students how these elements can improve their writing.

Step 2. Examine examples of enumerative, compare/contrast, and cause-and-effect paragraphs. Lead a think-aloud discussion on the characteristics of these paragraphs, emphasizing how each is structured. Provide students with additional paragraphs, and ask them to identify the textual format used in each. Discuss with students how the inclusion of different kinds of paragraphs can improve their writing.

Step 3. Describe the PLEASE strategy using the chart presented in Figure 4.2. Discuss with students the benefit of each step and when and where the strategy can be used. Ask students to examine one or more previously written papers. Discuss how the PLEASE strategy can strengthen what they currently do. Chart with the students how many parts (topic sentence, details, and concluding sentence) each included in one of their previously written paragraphs. Set a goal with students to learn and use the strategy.

Step 4. Model how to use the strategy to write each of the three different types of paragraphs: enumerative, compare/contrast, and cause and effect. Make the process of using the strategy visible by thinking out loud (see also Chapter 16). Encourage students to help you apply the strategy with each different type of paragraph. Discuss with students how the strategy helped you write good paragraphs. Identify the types of things you said that helped you use the strategy successfully. Encourage students to generate self-statements that will help them use the strategy.

Step 5. Describe why it is important to memorize the steps of the strategy ("so that you don't have to keep looking at the wall chart to remember the steps"). Ask students to work with a partner to memorize the steps of the strategy and any self-statements they plan to use.

Pick a topic.
List your ideas about the topic.
Evaluate your list.
Activate the paragraph with a topic sentence.
Supply supporting sentences.
End with a concluding sentence
            and
Evaluate your work.

Figure 4.2. The PLEASE strategy.

Tip 1: Some students do not need to memorize the steps of the strategy. They will learn them as they practice using it. Others will experience considerable difficulty remembering the steps. For these students, it is helpful to review and rehearse the steps at each session.

Tip 2: The first step of the PLEASE strategy, pick, prompts the students to identify the topic, paragraph format, and audience. When writing papers with multiple paragraphs, however, students do not need to identify the audience repeatedly. Teachers need to let students know this.

Tip 3: Not all paragraphs begin with a topic sentence, and many have no topic sentence at all. Once students have mastered the PLEASE strategy, we recommend that teachers introduce these alternative formats. One way to do this is to 1) identify a paragraph in children's reading material that corresponds to the selected alternative format, 2) write each sentence on a separate card, 3) shuffle the cards so that the sentences do not follow the original order, 4) direct students to make their own paragraph using the sentences, 5) ask students to compare their paragraph to the original, and 6) discuss the differences. Once students have done this with 10–15 examples, the teacher should model how to write a paragraph that follows the target structure. Students would then practice writing such paragraphs, receiving help as needed.

Step 6. Ask students to use the PLEASE strategy and their personal self-statements to write an enumerative paragraph. Provide them with any needed assistance. Encourage students to identify how the strategy and self-statements helped them write the paragraph. Ask them to see if they included all three parts of a paragraph (topic sentence, details, and concluding sentence). Have them chart the number of parts included, and compare this with their previous performance. Continue these steps until students can apply the strategy independently and successfully when writing an enumerative paragraph.

Step 7. Repeat Step 6 with compare/contrast and cause-and-effect paragraphs.

Step 8. Direct students to set a goal to use the strategy in the future, making a list of places and situations where it can be applied. Have them share with you or the class their successes and difficulties in applying the strategy. Identify ways to make the strategy more effective.

Step 9. Review periodically how to use the PLEASE strategy to write a good paragraph. This may include remodeling how to use the strategy, providing assistance in applying it, and generating opportunities where it can be applied.

What to Expect

The PLEASE strategy was validated with sixth-grade students with learning disabilities (Welch, 1992). All students had been identified by the participating school district as having learning disabilities. School criteria for identifying students who have learning disabilities included average intelligence and a significant discrepancy between ability and achievement. Students' scores on an individually administered test of intelligence ranged from 74 to 109, whereas their grade-level scores on an individually administered test of writing achievement ranged from 2.5 to 4.8.

Learning to use the PLEASE strategy had a positive effect on paragraph-writing skills (Welch, 1992). In comparison with students with learning disabilities who received instruction on basic writing skills (i.e., mechanics and grammar), students who were taught the strategy were more knowledgeable about the parts of a paragraph (reported effect size = .98), wrote better and more complete paragraphs (reported effect size = .51), and were more positive about their paragraph-writing ability (reported effect size = .47). Thus, the PLEASE strategy had a strong effect on students' knowledge and moderate effects on their paragraph-writing skills and attitudes.

Portability

The PLEASE strategy has only been tested with sixth-grade students with learning disabilities. Although we expect that it is applicable with other upper-elementary–grade students who experience difficulty with paragraph writing, we cannot recommend its use with younger children. In its present form, the strategy is probably too difficult for children in the primary grades.

Extensions

Two modifications would make the PLEASE strategy more useful for writing extended text. First, there is no need for students to stop at the end of each paragraph and use COPS to clean up mechanical miscues. This can be done more efficiently once the first draft is complete. Second, students need to learn how to design ending sentences that do more than simply rephrase the topic sentence. This includes learning how to generate ending sentences that provide a more comprehensive summary, showing succinctly how the major details and main ideas are linked together. It also includes learning how to construct ending sentences that serve as a gateway or linking statement to the next paragraph.

We end this chapter with another paragraph written by a child. The student was asked to write a paragraph about "people." PLEASE and COPS were not used to write this paragraph, but it does a good job of illustrating Mark Twain's observation that the "most interesting information comes from children." Who do you think wrote it? A boy or a girl?

> People are composed of girls and boys, also men and women. Boys are no good at all until they grow up and get married. Men who don't get married are no good either. Boys are an awful bother. They want everything they see except soap.

CHAPTER 5

PLANS

A Goal-Setting Strategy

Writing is often described as a problem-solving activity (Hayes & Flower, 1986; Scardamalia & Bereiter, 1986). When composing a report, for example, writers must develop a personal representation of what the task involves, identifying goals for their writing and ways of achieving them. These goals may be redefined or even cast aside during writing, and others may emerge as the writer struggles to bring task, goals, and content together in a coherent whole. These are the same kinds of processes—problem representation, goal setting, and so forth—that people use when trying to solve a wide range of problems.

If writing is problem solving, many of the tasks that writers must solve are best described as ill-defined problems. This point can be illustrated by examining a common school assignment, writing a report. For such an assignment, students often have vague or fuzzy notions as to what resources should be used to locate the needed information. They may be equally unsure of how many resources or references are needed. Finally, they often have no way of determining whether what they write is interesting or compelling.

Given the uncertain nature of writing, it should come as no surprise that advice on how to write ranges from the simplistic ("First have something to say, second say it, third stop when you have said it, and finally give it an accurate title"—nonfiction writer John Billings) to the sublime ("There are three rules for writing the novel; unfortunately no one knows what they are"—novelist W. Somerset Maugham) to the ridiculous ("Do not on any account attempt to write on both sides of the paper at once"—British authors W. Sellar and R. Yeatman). Fortunately, there are more effective means for dealing with an ill-defined problem. One is to do a means–end analysis (Flower &

Hayes, 1977). A means–end analysis involves figuring out what the final form of the paper will look like and determining the means by which the selected ends can be achieved. This helps students better define the writing assignment and make it more manageable.

A second approach is to break the writing problem into several subproblems. A writing assignment, for example, can be divided into the following components: 1) select a topic, 2) gain access to resources and generate notes, 3) organize notes, 4) write the paper, and 5) polish the paper by making final changes. By approaching the problem in this way, it becomes less overwhelming (Kellogg, 1987).

The *PLANS strategy* examined in this chapter is structured around a means–end analysis; students set product goals for what their paper will accomplish and articulate how these goals will be met. In addition, the writing task is broken down into several related subproblems revolving around the goal-setting process.

PLANS STRATEGY

The PLANS strategy breaks down the writing process into three related tasks (Graham, MacArthur, Schwartz, & Page-Voth, 1992). First, students develop a plan for writing their paper by selecting goals for what the paper will accomplish, specifying how they will meet these goals, and generating and organizing possible ideas for their paper. Second, students write the paper using their plan as a guide, expanding and reshaping the plan as they write. Third, they check to see whether their goals are met and make appropriate revisions if they are not. These three steps are described in more detail below.

Step 1. The processes involved in executing the first step of this strategy are encapsulated in the mnemonic PLANS. Each letter stands for a word or phrase that directs students' actions: *p*ick goals, *l*ist ways to meet goals, *a*nd make *n*otes, *s*equence notes. Students initiate planning by selecting goals from a list developed by the teacher (see PLANS worksheet, Figure 5.1). This list contains three sets of goals: one set for purpose, another for completeness, and a third for length. Students select a goal in each area and record their selection by placing a checkmark next to it. Next, they indicate on the PLANS worksheet how they will attain each goal. On a separate piece of paper, they generate ideas or notes for what their composition will say, keeping their goals in mind. Finally, they sequence the notes by placing a number next to what will come first, second, third, and so forth.

Step 2. During the second step, students use their plan (goals and notes) to write their paper. To remind them to continue the planning process of generating and organizing ideas as they write, they are encouraged to remind themselves to *write and say more*.

Step 3. Once the paper is completed, students check to see whether they met their goals. The original check placed by each selected goal is made into an "X" if the goal

---

1. PICK ONE GOAL FROM EACH SET

2. PLACE A CHECK BY EACH GOAL SELECTED

GOAL 1. PURPOSE

——— I will write a paper that convinces my friend that I am right.
——— I will write a paper that is fun for my friends to read.

Describe how I will accomplish the selected goal:

GOAL 2. PARTS

——— I will write a persuasive essay that has all of the parts.
——— I will write a story that has all of the parts.

Describe how I will accomplish the selected goal:

GOAL 3. LENGTH

——— I will write a paper that is 70 words long.
——— I will write a paper that is 90 words long.
——— I will write a paper that is 110 words long.
——— I will write a paper that is 130 words long.

Describe how I will accomplish the selected goal:

Note: Goals for length should be determined individually for each student; these numbers are only meant to be illustrative.

Figure 5.1.   PLANS worksheet with example goals for writing a persuasive essay and story.

is accomplished. If a goal is not obtained, the student considers how the paper can be revised to meet the objective. The new plan is then put into action. The words *test goals* are used to remind students to do this step.

It should be noted that the goals included in Figure 5.1 are limited to the goals we used as we initially tested the effectiveness of this strategy (Graham et al., 1992). Our approach to goal setting in this instance was to develop sets of goals and ask students to select one goal from each set. We believed that this participative approach was advantageous for three reasons. First, it reduced the complexity of the writing task by limiting the choice of goals to a manageable set of alternatives. Second, having the teacher select the goals helped to ensure that they were realistic (achievable by the student) and desirable (accomplishing the goals will improve the written product). Third, allowing students to make decisions about the selection of specific goals increased their ownership and commitment.

The astute reader will notice that the goals for "Purpose" in Figure 5.1 cannot be easily quantified or measured. Evaluating whether a story is fun to read or a persuasive essay is convincing is a subjective process. The inclusion of such goals runs counter to recommendations made later in Chapter 16, where we indicate that goals should be specific and relatively easy to measure. Although these goals are more vague than the other goals included in Figure 5.1, they are no less important. The judicious inclusion of general writing goals coupled with more specific product goals provides a much more comprehensive and broader net for casting one's writing plan.

Teaching the Strategy

General procedures for teaching PLANS using the SRSD model were described in Chapter 3. Only procedures specific to teaching this strategy are detailed here.

Students with learning disabilities, at least at the fifth-grade level, can learn to use the PLANS strategy in six to eight 40-minute sessions (4–6 hours total). We advise that students first learn to use PLANS with a single genre, such as persuasive writing. Once students can apply the strategy successfully and independently with one genre, we recommend that they then practice using it with a second one, then a third one, and so forth.

The need for our next suggestion is illustrated by a child's definition of *fibula* ("a small lie") and *celibacy* ("something you put in a salad"). Just as these words cannot be used appropriately unless their correct definition is known, the goals in Figure 5.1 cannot be met if students are unfamiliar with the meaning and fundamental concepts included in each objective. For example, to "write a persuasive essay with all the parts," students must know what a persuasive essay is and the basic elements included in one. Consequently, before learning the strategy, students learn about the purpose of persuasive writing, the elements included in such a composition, and how to identify and generate ideas for each of these parts. This includes locating each part in previously written essays as well as generating ideas for each part when given a persuasive essay prompt (e.g., "Should children your age be allowed to choose their own friends?"). The basic parts of a persuasive essay are topic sentence or premise, reasons to support the topic sentence, rebutting reasons for the other side, ending, and examples as well as elaborations.

Similarly, to meet the goal "write a paper that convinces my friend that I am right," students need to read and examine examples of essays that are particularly persuasive. This provides the students with concrete illustrations of how other authors have fulfilled this goal. Of course, the same essays can be used to demonstrate persuasiveness as well as basic parts.

A chart showing the PLANS strategy should be displayed where students can see it (see Figure 5.2). Students can also make their own personal chart to keep in their writing folder.

Step 1. Use **PLANS** to plan your paper.
Pick goals
List ways to meet goals
And make
Notes
Sequence notes

Step 2. Write and say more.

Step 3. Check to see that each goal was met.

Writing Better: Effective Strategies for Teaching Students with Learning Difficulties, by S. Graham and K.R. Harris, © 2005 Paul H. Brookes Publishing Co., Inc. All rights reserved.
Figure 5.2. The PLANS strategy.

As they learn to apply the strategy, some students will need help in selecting goals, deciding how they will meet their goals, establishing procedures for monitoring goal attainment, and revising their plans when a goal has not been achieved. These processes are discussed and modeled by the teacher. For example, different plans for achieving the goal "to include all the parts" can be modeled on successive days. Likewise, student application of these processes needs to be monitored closely. Teachers should provide hints and direct assistance whenever necessary.

What to Expect

The PLANS strategy was validated with fifth-grade students with learning disabilities (Graham et al., 1992). The students were taught to use the PLANS strategy to write persuasive essays. Their scores on an individually administered intelligence test ranged from 87 to 100 (all within the average range). Their reading performance on an individually administered achievement battery was 2 or more years below grade level. Teachers' claims that each student had difficulty with writing were confirmed by students' scores on an individually administered writing measure. Their writing scores on this test were 1 or more standard deviations below the mean.

Learning to use the PLANS strategy changed how these fifth-grade students wrote, improved what they wrote, and increased their knowledge about the process of writing (Graham et al., 1992). Before learning to use the strategy, the participating students did no planning in advance. After instruction, they averaged 8 minutes planning their papers, using all or most of the strategy steps specified by the PLANS mnemonic in Step 1. The *write and say more* prompt (Step 2) also appeared to be effective because 90% of all persuasive essays produced after instruction included additional details and ideas that were not included in students' initial plans.

Changes in how students wrote were accompanied by impressive changes in what they wrote. Their postinstruction essays were almost 2.5 times longer than the ones they wrote during baseline. Before instruction, only 21% of their papers contained all of the basic parts of a persuasive essay. This increased to 89% after instruction. Most important, the overall scores for the quality of the students' essays doubled after instruction.

Finally, there was a shift in students' conceptualizations of what constitutes good writing. Before instruction, they focused primarily on the mechanical aspects of writ-

---

Tip 1: Tom Wolfe, author of *The Bonfire of the Vanities*, was reportedly seen by a neighbor at 3:00 in the morning chanting, "I wrote 10,000 words today! I wrote 10,000 words today!" This prodigious feat deserved celebration. Likewise, you want to encourage your students to celebrate their accomplishments. When children achieve their goals, encourage them to do a little victory dance, place stars on their paper, or display their paper on the wall.

Tip 2: Product goals, such as those involving length, should be determined individually for each student. This can be done by examining several papers written before the strategy is introduced. An average for each paper is computed and the lowest goal is set 10% to 20% above the mean. Each succeeding goal increases by an equivalent amount.

Tip 3: Some students may need to start with just one or two goals and may find product goals easier to work with at first. In general, however, we recommend that students select no more than three to five goals and that at least one of these goals be a general writing goal.

---

ing (i.e., handwriting, spelling). After instruction, students were more likely to describe good writing in terms of substantive actions involving planning and content generation.

The two essays presented below illustrate how the strategy improved the writing performance of one student with learning disabilities. The essay written after instruction ended is clearly superior to the paper generated before instruction began (which, by the way, is about the advisability of children going to school in the summer). The second essay contains a clearly stated premise, two solid reasons to support the premise ("get fat" and "get a toothache"), and a concluding sentence. The text related to getting fat, however, could be improved through some simple resequencing. Spelling, punctuation, and capitalization errors were corrected for both compositions.

Before instruction:

No, because it will be too hot. And you will miss fun things and going swimming.

After instruction:

I think children should not be allowed to eat whatever they want. They will get fat and they might eat too much. Some of the calories are too high. They can get a toothache from sweets like cake, candy, and ice cream. That's why I believe that children should not be allowed to eat whatever they want.

Portability

The value of PLANS for students who do not have learning disabilities is unclear. There have been no scientific tests of its applicability beyond fifth-grade students with learning disabilities. We expect that the strategy would be effective with a wide variety of students for two reasons. First, generating and organizing ideas, two of the processes that PLANS helps students activate, are among the most basic writing processes (Hayes & Flower, 1986). Even with young novice writers, both of these processes can be enhanced through instruction (Scardamalia & Bereiter, 1986). Second, goal setting is a powerful tool for increasing performance (Locke et al., 1981), and setting product goals has improved the writing of students with and without learning disabilities in several other studies (see Chapter 16).

There is also some evidence that after learning to use the PLANS strategy with one genre, students with learning disabilities generalize its use to a second genre. This occurred for some of the fifth-grade students in the investigation by Graham and colleagues (1992). After learning to use PLANS to write persuasive essays, they applied part or all of the strategy when writing stories. The application of PLANS occurred even though they had not practiced using the strategy to write stories. Because this did not occur for all of the participating children, however, students should be directly taught to use the strategy with each new genre.

Extensions

There are three ways to extend the PLANS strategy. One way is to make the goals included on the PLANS worksheet (see Figure 5.1) address other aspects of writing, including

Specific attributes:	"I will write a paper that has four reasons to support my premise."
	"I will share with the reader four things about the main character."
Vocabulary:	"I will write a story containing 15 describing words."
Sentence variety:	"I will write a paper in which one fourth of the sentences are either compound or complex."
Mechanics:	"I will write a paper with no spelling errors."

These examples are not meant to be exhaustive, merely illustrative. Different goals can be included in each of these categories, and other categories are possible as well. Whenever a new untested goal is added to the PLANS worksheet, the teacher needs to assess its effectiveness.

Another extension of the PLANS strategy is to apply it with genres other than persuasive essay and story writing. It can be adapted so that it is appropriate for almost any genre. For example, two goals for writing a fable include "I will write a fable that has a good moral" and "I will write a fable that has all of the parts" (e.g., talking animals, dialogue, moral).

A third extension of PLANS is to the area of revising. The strategy can be modified so that the goals presented on the PLANS worksheet are for revising. For revising a story, the worksheet might be modified as shown in Figure 5.3.

---

1. SELECT ONE OR TWO GOALS FOR REVISING YOUR STORY

2. PLACE A CHECK BY EACH GOAL SELECTED

_____   I will include an additional character as part of the story.

_____   I will change the ending of the story to make it more exciting.

_____   I will change the time of the story to 150 years in the future.

_____   I will include a protagonist in the story who tries to stop the main character from achieving her or his goals.

_____   I will change the setting of the story to the planet Mars.

Describe how I will accomplish the selected goals:

Figure 5.3.   Modified PLANS worksheet for revising a story.

All of the revising goals require students to restructure their stories in some fundamental way, compelling them to make substantial changes in their papers. As a result, we recommend that students choose only one or two goals to work on at any given time. Of course, revising goals do not have to be this difficult. They could be as simple as "I will add five ideas that will improve my paper," "I will include an ending," or "I will tell how the main character feels at the end of the story." The selected revising goals should directly match each student's needs and writing maturity.

Once a student selects one or more revising goals, the strategy operates in much the same way as it does for planning. To illustrate, after picking the goal, "I will include an additional character as part of the story," the student decides who the new character is and how this character fits into the story. The student then records his or her plans for achieving this goal and makes notes about the character on the PLANS worksheet. The pertinent sections of the paper are rewritten, with the student reminding themselves to *write and say more* as they revise. After making changes, the student checks to see whether the goal was attained (*check to see that each goal was met*) and makes appropriate revisions if this was not the case.

CHAPTER 6

STOP and LIST

Goal Setting, Brainstorming, and Organizing

When planning the script for *Star Trek III: The Search for Spock*, Harve Bennett decided to pick up the action where the previous movie, *The Wrath of Khan*, left off. He established two goals that he wanted to resolve while writing: What did Spock's dying remark, "Remember," mean? What would happen if the Klingons learned that the Genesis technology could destroy as well as create life? Focusing on these goals, he generated and organized ideas into an outline that served as his initial plan for the movie.

These same three actions—goal setting, generating ideas, and organizing ideas—are the prime ingredients for planning written text (Hayes & Flower, 1986). Good writers commonly set goals to guide the writing process, generating and organizing writing content to meet their objectives. The strategy presented in this chapter applies this same basic structure. Students establish one or more overarching goals for their papers and brainstorm possible ideas before writing, selecting and sequencing what they plan to use (Troia & Graham, 2002; Troia, Graham, & Harris, 1999). This provides an initial but flexible roadmap that students enlarge, modify, restructure, or even trim while writing.

STOP AND LIST STRATEGY

The *STOP and LIST* mnemonic serves as a reminder for students to set goals, generate possible writing ideas, and sequence these ideas before writing.

Step 1. STOP: The first word reminds students to stop and set goals (i.e., establish their purpose for writing). Each letter of this mnemonic stands for a word in the phrase: *s*top and *t*hink *of p*urposes. Examples of purposes or goals include "Write a funny story to share during writing time" or "Write directions on how to play checkers." Students record their purposes for writing at the top of a planning sheet (see Figure 6.1).

Step 2. LIST: The second word reminds students to generate and organize ideas. Again each letter stands for a word that directs students' behavior: *l*ist *i*deas and *s*equence *t*hem. When listing ideas, students brainstorm possible writing content for their paper. Keeping their writing topic and goals in mind, students generate as many ideas as they can, recording each on their planning sheet (see Figure 6.1). Next, they examine these ideas, select the ones they plan to include in their paper, and sequence them by numbering which will come first, second, third, and so forth. They cross out any ideas they decide not to include in their paper.

Step 3. Students use this writing plan to guide their composing efforts. They are encouraged to continue the process of planning while writing. This process includes adding new ideas to the plan, expanding existing points, culling redundant or unimportant details, and modifying the organizational structure.

Stop   Purposes:

Think   1.

Of   2.

Purposes   3.

and

      List   **I**deas   **S**equence   **T**hem

_____

_____

_____

_____

_____

_____

_____

_____

Remember: Decide which ideas to use and show their sequence by numbering them.

Figure 6.1.   Planning sheet for STOP and LIST.

Tip 1: Some children with learning disabilities may experience difficulty generating appropriate goals or purposes for their compositions. One way of addressing this problem is to provide them with a set of goals to choose from as they are learning to use the STOP and LIST strategy. As they become more confident and familiar with goal setting, the teacher can gradually fade this assistance.

Tip 2: Some students may forget to use one or more of the ideas they included on their STOP and LIST planning sheet (see Figure 6.1). To help ensure that they include all of the intended content, ask them to place a checkmark next to each idea as they include it in their paper.

Tip 3: When asked what to do before help arrived for a man with a head wound, a child replied, "I would put a tourniquet around his neck." Like the tourniquet in this dubious suggestion, the STOP and LIST planning sheet is only a temporary aid. A planning sheet such as this will not be available every time students write. Once students have mastered the strategy, the use of the planning sheet should be faded, and they should set their goals, brainstorm, and sequence ideas on regular paper.

Teaching the Strategy

An illustration of how to teach the STOP and LIST strategy was presented in Chapter 3 (see Example 3: Teaching STOP and LIST); it is not repeated here. Students with learning disabilities, at least at the fourth- and fifth-grade level, typically require between 9 and 11 hours of instruction to master this strategy. We advise that students first learn to use STOP and LIST with a single genre such as story writing. Once students can apply the strategy successfully and independently with one genre, they then practice using it with a second one, and so forth. STOP and LIST is likely to be more effective if students are already familiar with the characteristics of the target genre. Thus, before teaching the strategy, these elements are taught or reviewed. For example, if students are learning to use the strategy to write stories, they might first read several well-written stories. The teacher and students would then identify what makes these stories exceptional, emphasizing that including these elements in one's own stories will result in better writing.

What to Expect

The STOP and LIST strategy was validated with fourth- and fifth-grade students with learning disabilities in two separate studies. In the first study, fifth-grade students with learning disabilities were taught to use the strategy to write stories (Troia et al., 1999). These students' scores on an individually administered intelligence test were slightly greater than 100, but their achievement on individually administered measures of reading and writing were 1 standard deviation (*SD*) or more below the mean. In addition to special education services, two of the three students participating in this study also received speech and language therapy.

Learning to use the STOP and LIST strategy changed not only what these fifth-grade students with learning disabilities wrote but their approach to composing as well. Before learning to use the strategy, the participating students did no planning in advance of writing (Troia et al., 1999). After instruction, they typically spent 20 minutes or more planning their stories, generating almost 19 possible ideas for their papers. This increased attention to advanced planning resulted in an almost 150% increase in the length of their compositions. There was a similar improvement in the completeness and breadth of their papers, as the number of basic story elements increased by almost 150%. Although improvements in overall story quality were minimal immediately after instruction, this was not the case 3 weeks later. By this point, quality scores had improved by 135%.

In the second study, fourth- and fifth-grade students with learning disabilities were taught to use STOP and LIST to write stories. These students' scores on an individually administered intelligence test were generally in the average range (i.e., IQ scores ranged from 80 to 135; mean = 109). All students had an individualized education program goal to improve writing, and their writing difficulties were further confirmed by their performance on an individually administered achievement measure. All of the participating children's writing scores on this test were 1 or more *SD* below the mean.

In the second study (Troia & Graham, 2002), the findings were not as dramatic for planning but followed the same basic pattern. Students increased their average planning time from 9 seconds during baseline to 6 minutes after instruction. At this point, they generated five ideas for their stories. The effects of the strategy on overall writing quality were quite marked, however. In comparison with more traditional process writing instruction (Graves, 1983), the STOP and LIST strategy resulted in qualitatively better stories immediately after instruction (effect size = 1.00) and 1 month later (effect size = 2.05).

The impact of STOP and LIST on the writing of students with learning disabilities is illustrated in the two stories that follow. The first was written before instruction and the second after students had learned to use the strategy. Spelling, capitalization, and punctuation errors were corrected in both. It should be noted that before the pre-instruction story was collected, students had been taught to identify and generate ideas for each of the basic parts of a story. Consequently, both of the stories below include a setting and complete episodes.

Before instruction:

Once upon a time, there was [a] pirate ship. It was just built a few weeks before it set sail. Everybody was really excited about the ship, but it was winter and it was very cold, and some people did not want to go. There was a kid by the name of Mark. He really wanted to go on the voyage but he had a problem. He couldn't just go, there were tryouts. The rules were [that] there was a race between everybody who wants to tryout. So Mark practiced and practiced for 5 hours a day for a week.

When it was time for the race, Mark was ready. The gun sounded and they were racing, Mark and the two other boats were tied for first. They raced for 2 hours. Finally, they reached the finish line. Mark had won by a foot. Mark was going on the voyage. He was very happy and proud.

After instruction:

Jackson's Life in the 1700s

He never really wanted to be a sailor, but he did so because he was running away from troubles. He was a volunteer, most sailors were. His name was Jackson and he lived in a lower class town almost all of his life. On his first voyage to the New World, he felt sad and disappointed. He was a little excited to go to the New World, but not enough to make him a sailor for that reason. No, it was those troubles. He had no family back in England. No wife. No parents, that is, no parents that raised him [properly]. It was just that his mother gave birth to him and then the rest was [up] to him. He had raised himself. As for his father, he was a drunk, never proud of him, carrying more for his bottles of scotch.

At Jackson's first voyage, a huge tidal wave struck the boat and set it way off course. If it was not for a gust of wind, the boat would have gone back to England. After 3 nights' voyage, a group of sailors were drinking. Pip, who was one of the sailors, refused the alcohol and went to his cabin. When they asked Jackson, he remembered that scotch was [a] very addictive kind of alcohol, along with rum. So he said no also. Later that night four of those drinkers jumped off the boat and into the sea. Jackson was glad he didn't have any.

Five months later, land was sighted and the [boat] set ashore. He was relieved from all of the troubles he had got away from when he was in England. Jackson spent 15 years in the New World and had a good life. When he heard about the West, Jackson ventured onto the Oregon Trail.

Portability

The value of the STOP and LIST strategy for students without learning disabilities is unclear. There have been no scientific tests of its applicability beyond fourth- and fifth-grade students with learning disabilities. We expect that the strategy would be effective with younger students with learning disabilities and for other students who do little or no advance planning when writing for two reasons. First, goal setting, brainstorming, and sequencing are among the most basic planning processes in writing (Hayes & Flower, 1986). Second, we have seen struggling writers learn to use at least two of these processes, brainstorming and sequencing, as early as first and second grade.

There is also some evidence that after learning to use STOP and LIST with one genre, students with learning disabilities generalize its use to a second genre. This occurred for the fifth-grade students in the investigation by Troia and colleagues (1999). The students were only taught how to use the strategy to write stories, but they were also able to use it to write persuasive essays, resulting in longer and more complete papers. Teachers should not assume that such transfer will always occur, however, because it was not evident with the fourth- and fifth-grade students with learning disabilities in the other Troia and Graham (2002) study. Instead, students should be directly taught to use the strategy with each new genre.

Extensions

When extending the use of STOP and LIST to a new genre, such as persuasive writing, we recommend the following steps.

Step 1. Teach students the characteristics of the genre with which they will use STOP and LIST. Ask students to read several model compositions that illustrate the basic characteristics of the genre. Identify and discuss these characteristics with students, emphasizing that including these elements in their papers will result in better writing.

Step 2. Tell students how STOP and LIST can improve their writing with the target genre. This can include examining previously written papers to show where the strategy will strengthen what they currently do.

Step 3. Model how to use the strategy to write a paper in the target genre. Ask students to help you set goals, brainstorm ideas, and sequence them. After writing the paper, discuss how the strategy helped you write a better paper.

Step 4. Ask students to use STOP and LIST to write two or more papers in the target genre. Provide them with any needed assistance. Initially, you might have students work together as they use the strategy to write a paper. Have students identify how the strategy helped them write better. Ask them to compare their current papers with ones they wrote before using STOP and LIST. This step continues until the student can apply the strategy independently.

Step 5. Direct students to set a goal to use the strategy, making a list of places and situations where they can apply it when working on the target genre. Have them share with you or the class their successes and difficulties in applying the strategy. Identify ways to make their use of the strategy more effective.

Step 6. Review periodically how to use STOP and LIST to write a paper in the target genre. This may include remodeling how to use the strategy, providing assistance in applying it, and generating opportunities where it can be applied.

Step 7. Evaluate the effectiveness of your instruction and the impact of the strategy using the assessment guidelines contained in Chapter 17.

Another possible extension of the STOP and LIST strategy involves modifying how the brainstorming and organizing components operate. Shelby Foote, a historian and contributor to Ken Burns's PBS documentary on the Civil War, demonstrated one way to do this. He recorded and organized his notes on the Civil War by drawing four columns down large cardboard posters. One column was for diplomacy, a second for politics, a third for military, and a fourth for miscellaneous items. Under each column, he entered his notes chronologically for each year of the Civil War. This allowed him to tell at a glance what was happening at a given point in time, making it easier to weave the political, military, and diplomatic situations into a single narrative.

Foote's strategy is commonly known as *concept mapping*. It involves visually organizing information by categories (Washington, 1988). A popular version of concept mapping is semantic webbing. With this technique, students write the key concept, for example, *dragon*, in the middle of the page and circle it. They then brainstorm possible related ideas or questions such as, What do they eat? Where do they live? What do they like to do? How can you find them? Each related idea or question is abbreviated (e.g., Like To Do?), circled, and placed at equal intervals around the key concept or central bubble (i.e., dragon). The students connect each related bubble (e.g., Like To Do?) to the central one with a line, showing their relationship. They then brainstorm or generate ideas for each related idea or question (e.g., eats people, hoards gold, breathes fire, destroys villages). The ideas are placed in abbreviated form around the bubble for the pertinent question and connected to it with a short line.

Instead of brainstorming and sequencing ideas by numbering them as is currently done in STOP and LIST, students can alternatively brainstorm and web ideas. One possible advantage to this approach is that students not only organize their ideas categorically, but they also can see the connections between them more readily (as did Shelby Foote). As with other recommended extensions, however, teachers need to carefully monitor the effectiveness of this modification (see Chapter 17). Despite the widespread popularity of semantic webbing, its effects on the writing of students with learning disabilities have only been tested at the middle-school level (with a positive impact, we are happy to report; see Strum & Rankin-Erickson, 2002).

CHAPTER 7

The Peer Revising Strategy

Revising is particularly effective because it allows writers to correct their mistakes. Consider the consequences of the following directions before they were amended.

> *Important Notice:* If you are one of the hundreds of parachuting enthusiasts who bought our Easy Sky Diving book, please make the following correction on page 8, line 7. The words "state zip code" should read "pull rip cord."

Kurt Vonnegut, the author of *Slaughterhouse-Five*, provided another reason for revising, noting that anyone can write well "if only that person will write the same thought over and over again, improving it a little each time." Or as the novelist Robert Cormier put it, "The beautiful part of writing is that you don't have to get it right the first time, unlike, say, a brain surgeon." Stephen King, the horror writer, seconded this sentiment: "Only God gets it right the first time."

How then can teachers get students with learning disabilities to revise more frequently and skillfully? One solution is *peer response*: Peers read each other's papers and provide suggestions for improving them. This makes the audience an integral part of the writing process, allowing the writer to get advanced feedback from one or more readers. By interacting directly with the audience, the writer becomes more conscious of the needs of the readers.

The revising strategy presented in this chapter is centered around peer response. Peers provide suggestions to each other on how to improve their first drafts using a specific strategy and selected evaluation criteria. We believe that the combination of peer response and strategy instruction is an especially powerful procedure. Strategy instruction provides students with an explicit framework for responding to a peer's writing. Peer response provides a motivating social context for using the strategy, as peers work together to improve their writing.

Evaluation of other students' writing using specific criteria is also beneficial, because it helps children acquire knowledge about how to write (Hillocks, 1986). By actively applying criteria, such as clarity or detail, to evaluate other students' writing, children gain knowledge about what is important in writing. This new knowledge is then used to guide their own production of future compositions. Focusing attention on substantive issues such as clarity and detail further increases the likelihood that students will make revisions that affect the meaning of what they write.

PEER REVISING STRATEGY

The peer revising strategy (MacArthur, Schwartz, & Graham, 1991) includes two parts: one in which revising focuses on substance (*Revise*) and a second in which revising concentrates on mechanical issues (*Edit*). The steps for Revise are presented in Figure 7.1; Edit is summarized in Figure 7.2. The teacher assigns each student a writing partner. The author of a paper is called the *writer*. The student providing feedback on the paper is called the *listener*. The steps for Revise and Edit are written from the perspective of the listener.

Once a writer finishes the first draft of a paper, Revise is initiated by sharing the paper with the listener. First, the writer reads the paper aloud while the listener reads along. Active listening is stressed, and the listener is encouraged to ask questions about anything that is unclear. The read-along arrangement ensures that the listener knows what the writer wrote. Some listeners will not be able to read the writer's paper unaided because of limited reading skills or because of writing errors involving handwriting, spelling, punctuation, or sentence construction.

After the paper is read, the listener tells the writer what the paper is about and what she or he liked best. This helps ensure that the listener pays attention and starts the peer response process off on a positive note. In telling what the paper is about, the listener is encouraged to comment on main ideas or important parts.

Next, the listener reads the writer's paper, asking for help from the writer if a particular part of the paper cannot be read. While reading, the listener asks two questions: "Is

---

The Listener's Job: Revising

Step 1. Listen and read along as the writer reads the paper.
Step 2. Tell what the paper is about and what you liked best.
Step 3. Read the paper and make notes: **Is everything clear?**
                                                Can any details be added?
Step 4. Share your suggestions with the writer.

Figure 7.1.   Chart for the revise strategy.

The Listener's Job: Editing

Step 1. Check the writer's paper for errors in: **Sentences**

                                                          Capitals

                                                          Punctuation

                                                          Spelling

Step 2. Share your suggestions with the writer.

Writing Better: Effective Strategies for Teaching Students with Learning Difficulties, by S. Graham and K.R. Harris,
© 2005 Paul H. Brookes Publishing Co., Inc. All rights reserved.
Figure 7.2.   Chart for the edit strategy.

there anything that is not clear?" and "Is there any place where more detail can be added?" If a part is hard to understand, a question mark is placed next to it. The listeners are asked to make at least three suggestions for things the writer can say more about. These suggestions are written directly on the paper, using carets to indicate where they go.

The two students then get back together to discuss the listener's recommendations. The listener is encouraged to make specific suggestions for executing the recommended changes. The writer asks questions about anything that is not clear. The writer then revises the paper, using the listener's suggestions. The writer does not have to use all of the suggestions, only those that he or she believes will make the paper better.

The second part of the strategy, Edit, involves correcting errors. Before returning their revised paper to the listener, writers check their own paper, correcting any errors they find. Students use the checklist in Figure 7.3 to complete this task.

Once a writer checks his or her paper, it is given to the listener who uses the checklist in Figure 7.3 to mark and correct any errors missed by the writer. The two students get back together and discuss any corrections made by the listener.

Sentences:	Is each sentence complete?
Capitals:	Are first letters of sentences capitalized? Are proper nouns capitalized?
Punctuation:	Is there punctuation at the end of each sentence?
Spelling:	Circle words you are not sure of and correct with a spell-checker or a dictionary.

Writing Better: Effective Strategies for Teaching Students with Learning Difficulties, by S. Graham and K.R. Harris,
© 2005 Paul H. Brookes Publishing Co., Inc. All rights reserved.
Figure 7.3.   Checklist for correcting errors.

Teaching the Strategy

The general procedures used to teach the peer revising strategy are presented in Chapter 3. As a result, only procedures specific to teaching this strategy are provided here.

First, it is easier to use the peer revising strategy if students do their composing on the computer instead of by hand. With this strategy, a child's paper is marked by the listener when feedback is provided during Revise and Edit. Papers are also written on when the writer corrects mechanical miscues during Edit or when other changes are made during the writing process. Unless the student is willing to recopy the paper on one or more occasions (many students with learning disabilities resist this), it can become so messy that even the writer cannot read it. Composing on the computer makes it easy for the writer to make neat copies each time revisions are made, eliminating the tedious and time-consuming process of recopying by hand.

When teaching the peer revising strategy, we first teach students Revise, and once they have mastered this process, Edit is taught. This is done for two reasons. First, it focuses students' attention on the importance of substance right from the start. Second, it makes learning the strategy easier because only one part is taught at a time.

As teachers demonstrate how to use the strategy (i.e., Model It), we find it especially beneficial to show students a videotape of two peers executing the strategy. Seeing other children perform the strategy reinforces students' beliefs that they can do it as well. Teachers who cannot make such a videotape can have two writers who already know how to use the strategy model it for the class.

Our final instructional caveat is illustrated in the following letter to a sick child.

Dear Erika,

I hope you get well soon.
Mrs. Dickey forced us to write this letter.
So I'm not writing it because I like you.

Your friend, Leon.

Children's interactions are not always positive. Teachers need to emphasize that feedback and suggestions are to be delivered in a positive manner. Furthermore, as students practice applying the strategy (i.e., Support It), each child needs to practice being both the writer and the listener. At first, especially with younger children, the teacher needs to provide the listener with considerable help in responding to the writer's paper. This includes providing hints as to what parts of the paper are unclear or lacking in detail. It may also involve re-modeling how to use the strategy.

What to Expect

The peer revising strategy was validated with fourth- through sixth-grade students with learning disabilities as they wrote and revised narrative text (MacArthur, Schwartz, & Graham, 1991). Each student's score on an individually administered intelligence test was in the average range (i.e., 85–115). All students' achievement on individually administered measures of reading and writing, however, was at least 1.5 years below grade level. None of the students was receiving other special education services and all of them spoke English proficiently.

When fourth- through sixth-grade students with learning disabilities used the peer revising strategy, it not only changed their revising behavior but also had a positive effect on what they wrote (MacArthur et al., 1991). In comparison with students in a

Tip 1: A student describing his anatomy class the year before sheepishly indicated that he was the "chairman of the hindbone section." He clearly saw this as an inferior position. It is important that students act as equal partners when working on classroom projects as well as when using the peer revising strategy. Students paired together should not only be compatible but able to work together cooperatively without getting off-task.

Tip 2: One of the more unique descriptions of Hamlet that we have heard is that he "was a small pig made famous by Shakespeare." Just as the reader needs to understand who the characters are in Shakespeare's plays, students using peer revising need to grasp when and why they revise. "We revise and edit our papers before they are published in our writing book, posted on the writing board, or shared with a broader audience such as the principal, kids from other classes, or our parents. We revise so that our writing makes sense and to make it as good as it can be." This places revising and the strategy in the larger context of the full writing process.

Tip 3: Students who write their papers by hand should be encouraged to triple space. This will provide plenty of room for feedback from the reader and for the writer to make revisions.

more traditional process writing program (Graves, 1983), children who used the peer revising strategy made almost three times as many revisions (effect size = 1.29), and almost twice as many revisions involved words, phrase, and larger units of text (effect size = .64). The strategy had a strong impact on the overall quality of students' text (effect size = 1.19) and a moderate impact on decreasing spelling errors (effect size = .54). Students reduced spelling miscues by 40% from first to second draft. Furthermore, students who learned to use the strategy internalized the evaluation criteria included in Revise because they identified these elements when asked to define *good writing* and *revising*.

Portability

The specific peer response strategy presented here has not been scientifically tested with elementary-age students beyond fourth- through sixth-grade students with learning disabilities (see MacArthur et al., 1991). There is good reason to believe, however, that this strategy can be applied broadly, at least with children without disabilities. In a series of studies, children in general education classrooms ages 6–11 were taught to use a peer planning and revising strategy (Nixon & Topping, 2001; Sutherland & Topping, 1999; Yarrow & Topping, 2001). Use of the strategy resulted in improved writing for all age groups. The revising part of the strategy used in these studies shared many similarities with the peer revising strategy described in this chapter. Both strategies involved the writer and listener reading the first draft, the listener providing feedback involving substance and form, and the pair discussing these suggestions. It is important to note that no attempt was made to determine the unique impact of either the planning or revising strategies in these studies. Thus, any application of peer revising to students other than fourth- through sixth-grade children with learning disabilities should be carefully monitored (see Chapter 17).

Extensions

One way to extend the peer revising strategy is by adding, substituting, or even removing one or more of the evaluation criteria included in Revise or Edit (see Stoddard & MacArthur, 1993). For example, in the version of the peer revising strategy presented here, the listener asks questions about clarity and detail. The complexity of the strategy can be increased by adding other criteria involving attributes such as completeness (e.g., Does it have a good beginning, middle, or ending?) or organization (e.g., Does the paper follow a logical sequence?). Likewise, the strategy can be made easier by eliminating one or more criteria.

Another way to modify the strategy is to match the evaluation criteria more specifically to the type of paper students are writing. If students are learning to write fiction, for example, the evaluation criteria might focus on the character (e.g., Do you need to know more about the main character?) or other common aspects of a story. Regardless of which modification is made, teachers need to carefully monitor the success of any new evaluation criteria on students' writing (see Chapter 17).

CHAPTER 8

The CDO Revising Strategy

"You should have seen the first draft." Just like the fish that got away, this is a common excuse that editors give when a book is either poorly written or edited. Revising is at the heart of good writing. The Russian novelist Vladimir Nabokov once claimed, "My pencils outlast their erasers." A similar idea was expressed by Leo Tolstoy, another Russian novelist, who claimed that an author must be two people, writer and critic.

Despite its importance, revising is not easy. Theodore Geisel (also known as Dr. Seuss, the author of the beloved *Cat in the Hat* books) indicated, "I know my stuff all looks like it was rattled off in 23 seconds, but every word is a struggle." Revising is so important that some writers just can't give it up. Walt Whitman kept revising *Leaves of Grass* until he was 73, and John Fowles published a revised edition of *The Magus* 12 years after the first edition.

Revising is also difficult for young writers (Graham & Harris, 2003a; Scardamalia & Bereiter, 1986) because it involves the coordination of several complex processes (Scardamalia & Bereiter, 1983, 1985b). Revising may be initiated when writers discover a mismatch between their intentions and what they actually wrote. Revising may also occur because the writer thought of something better to say or decided that some part of the text might be too difficult for the reader. Because revising may occur for different reasons, it is not surprising that writers use different strategies for making changes. In some instances, the writer decides what is wrong before initiating the revision. In other cases, the writer makes a revision without bothering to figure this out. In either situation, the writer must decide what to do—add, rewrite, delete, or move text—and how to do it.

The *CDO revising strategy* provides a framework that helps children orchestrate the revising process (Scardamalia & Bereiter, 1983). The strategy ensures that the separate elements of revising are coordinated and occur in a regular way. The CDO acronym stands for *compare*, *diagnose*, and *operate*. *Compare* involves identifying where a revision is needed, *diagnose* determines the problem, and *operate* specifies and executes the intended revision. Furthermore, CDO helps students with learning disabilities to move beyond the thesaurus approach to revising that they typically use (De La Paz, Swanson, & Graham, 1998) because the criteria that students use during *diagnose* focus on substance and not form.

CDO REVISING STRATEGY

The CDO revising strategy (Graham, 1997) involves revising a paper sentence by sentence, starting with the first sentence and proceeding on to the final one (see Figure 8.1). After reading a sentence (Step 1. Compare), the student selects an evaluation card that best describes it (Step 2. Diagnose).

One of the cards (*This is not useful to my paper*) asks writers to consider the sentence in relation to the overall purpose of the paper. Two other cards (*This doesn't sound right*; *People may not understand this part*) focus on the clarity of the sentence, bidding writers to both analyze and listen to the sentence to identify parts that may confuse readers. Another card (*This is not what I intended to say*) helps writers identify any mismatches between what they intended to say and what was actually said. Two additional cards (*People won't be interested in this part*; *People won't believe this part*) prompt writers to evaluate readers' reactions to the sentence. The final card (*This is good*) indicates that the sentence does not need to be revised.

Each evaluation statement should be printed on a white card with a green border. The color green reminds students to start with these cards. The words *Evaluate each sentence* should also be printed at the top of each card to remind students that they are assessing each sentence.

Step 1.	**Compare:**	Read the sentence.
Step 2.	**Diagnose:**	Select the best evaluation cards.
		This doesn't sound right.
		This is not what I intended to say.
		This is not useful to my paper.
		This is good.
		People may not understand this part.
		People won't be interested in this part.
		People won't believe this part.
Step 3.	**Operate:**	Select a tactic card.
		Rewrite.
		Add more.
		Leave this part out.
		Change the wording.
Step 4.	**Operate:**	Make your revision.

Figure 8.1.   Chart for the CDO strategy.

Whenever an evaluation card other than *This is good* is selected, students first think about how to correct the problem, then choose one of five tactic cards (Step 3. Operate), and finally carry out the intended revision (Step 4. Operate). The tactic cards direct students to *Rewrite, Add more, Leave this part out,* or *Change the wording.* Also, each revising tactic should be typed on a white card with a red border to signal that this is the final step in making a revision.

Teaching the Strategy

The steps used by Graham (1997) to teach the CDO strategy are presented below. Students were able to independently use the strategy (with cards and a wall chart; see Figure 8.1) after a single 30-minute session.

Step 1. The teacher and students discuss the importance of revising (e.g., "to make your paper better").

Step 2. The teacher tells students she is going to teach a strategy that will help them revise better. She describes the strategy using the wall chart pictured in Figure 8.1. Students are encouraged to ask questions about the strategy.

Step 3. The teacher models how to use the strategy on a previously written paper. She asks students to help her select appropriate evaluation and tactic cards as she assesses each sentence.

Step 4. Each student is given a short text sample and is asked to demonstrate that he or she can use the CDO strategy independently. The teacher provides any assistance needed and helps students until the students can use the strategy by themselves. To be maximally effective, however, we recommend that the CDO strategy be taught using the self-regulated strategy instruction (SRSD) procedures described in Chapter 3. This includes presenting the rationale underlying each evaluation criterion, making sure that students know what is meant by each of the tactical operations (e.g., rewrite), discussing when and where to use the strategy, providing extended practice in applying the strategy (with teacher guidance and assistance), asking students to examine how the strategy improves their revising, setting goals to use the strategy, and conducting booster sessions to review the strategy and strengthen its use.

What to Expect

CDO was validated with fifth- and sixth-grade students with learning disabilities as they wrote and revised a story (Graham, 1997). Each student's score on an individually administered intelligence test was at or above the average range (i.e., 85 or greater). Each student's performance on an individually administered measure of reading was 2–4 years below grade level. Teachers' claims that the participating students experienced difficulty learning to write were confirmed by their performance on an individually administered measure of writing. Their average scores were 1 *standard deviation* below the nor-

Tip 1: A child revised the sentence "The bull and cow is in the field" to read "The cow and bull is in the field." When the frustrated teacher asked the student why she had made this change, she curtly replied, "Ladies come first." Not all of the criteria that students use to evaluate their writing are appropriate or successful. Teachers should carefully monitor the effectiveness of the evaluation criteria used in Step 2 of the CDO procedure. If a criterion is not effective, it should be removed or replaced. For example, we found that when students selected the criterion *This is not useful to my paper*, 100% of the revisions they made to correct this problem had a negative impact on that piece of text (Graham, 1997). On the other hand, the criterion *This doesn't sound right* resulted in improved text 65% of the times when selected.

Tip 2: Once students can use CDO strategy fluently and independently, the evaluation and tactic cards can be eliminated. Instead, students can be encouraged to use a smaller and personal version of the wall chart presented in Figure 8.1. This chart should be kept in students' writing folder.

Tip 3: Students who write their papers by hand should be encouraged to double- or triple-space. This will provide plenty of room for them to make revisions.

mative sample on this test. None of the students was receiving other special education services, and all of them spoke English proficiently.

When these students used the CDO revising strategy, they revised more frequently and more skillfully. In comparison with how they normally revised, there was a 134% increase in the number of revisions made. This increase occurred for revisions involving both substance (effect size = .38) and mechanics (effect size = .42). More important, the substantive revisions they made improved considerably (effect size = .83). It is important to note that these changes in revising behavior did not result in improvements in overall text quality. This is probably because the CDO strategy focuses students' attention on local rather than more global issues.

The effects of the CDO strategy on the revising behavior of students with learning disabilities are illustrated in these two drafts of a story written by a fifth-grade child. With the exception of a few minor word deletions and changes in punctuation, revisions were underlined in the second draft.

First Draft

Once upon a time there was a girl in Fourth grade. Her name was Joan. Her parents decided to get Joan a tutor. Joan hated the idea! The first day the tutor was coming Joan didn't like this is this is how the lesson happened.

Write when the tutor came she looked nice and sweet but shen she got into Joans room she got beety eyes and said "you wreched child".

I didn't now what I had done. After that lessone I was scared out of my whitts. 4 lessons had gone by with writing so many stories. When she came she told me the story and said "Write" So I started to write while she smoked in the middle of the writing nonsense the pen started to move. and wrote a whole story For me not every time she comes I just stare at the pen doing my work.

Second Draft

Once upon a time there was a girl in Fourth grade. Her name was Joan. Her parents saw that her grades were dropping. So her parents decided to get Joan a tutor. Joan hated the idea! The first day the tutor came Joan didn't want to go through with it. This is how the lesson went.

Write when the tutor came she looked nice and sweet, but when she got into Joans room she got beety eyes and said "you wreched child". I didn't now what to do. After that lessone I was scared to go to other lessons. 4 lessons had gone by with writing so many never ending stories. The next time she came she told me to "Write." So I started to write while she smoked. In the middle of writing nonsense, the pen started to move. and wrote the whole story For me. Now every time she comes I just stare at the pen doing my work.

In this story, the student made changes mainly by reworking the wording of sentences and by adding information. The two places in the first draft that were most confusing (the last sentence in each paragraph) were cleaned up by doing some minor reworking and adding punctuation. The child also changed verbs like *decided* and *was coming* to *saw* and *came*, making the story more active.

Portability

The CDO procedure appears to be a useful tool for fourth- through sixth-grade children in general classrooms. Scardamalia and Bereiter (1983) found that when these students used this strategy, they made more revisions than normal. In addition, the number of changes for the better exceeded the number of detrimental changes. As in the study with students with learning disabilities (Graham, 1997), however, these positive changes in revising behavior were not strong enough to enhance the overall quality of their text.

We cannot recommend the use of CDO with younger students for two reasons. First, it is a relatively cumbersome and complex procedure. Second, procedures such as the peer-revising strategy presented in Chapter 7 are more appropriate for younger writers who may have considerable difficulty evaluating the text from the point of view of the reader. The evaluation criteria in the CDO procedure ask students to evaluate sentences from both the writer's (e.g., "This is not what I wanted to say") and reader's (e.g., "People won't believe this part") perspectives.

Extensions

Some children are natural born revisers. When a Mom was showing off her new car, a Pontiac Grand Am, to her family, her young son indignantly exclaimed, "They misspelled Grandma." Because the evaluation criteria used in the version of CDO presented in Figure 8.1 focus solely on substance, some children (e.g., the child above) may start to get the message that they no longer need to focus on form. If this happens, the teacher can add evaluation cards that concentrate on the mechanics of writing (e.g., *Words are misspelled*).

The CDO strategy can also be extended by adding, substituting, or eliminating other evaluation or tactic cards. For example, teachers can make the strategy easier for some students by eliminating the evaluation criteria that focus on the reader's perspective.

- People may not understand this part.
- People won't be interested in this part.
- People won't buy this part.

Likewise, the complexity of the strategy can be geared upward by adding tactic cards:

- Give an example.
- Move this part.

Another way to modify the strategy is to match the evaluation criteria more specifically to the type of paper students are writing. If students are learning to write a persuasive essay, for example, the following evaluation cards might be included:

- This is a weak idea.
- This idea does not support my belief.

Regardless of which modification is made, teachers need to carefully monitor the success of any new evaluation or tactic cards on students' revising and writing behavior (see Chapter 17).

A final possible extension of the CDO strategy is for students to use it while they are writing a first draft (Scardamalia & Bereiter, 1983). After each sentence—or a section of text—is written, students stop and execute the CDO routine. The advantage of using the process "on line" is that students are encouraged to evaluate and revise as they write. The disadvantage is that this may (at least initially) disrupt the planning process, especially the generation of ideas.

CHAPTER 9

Summarizing Written Text

When asked about reading, Erskine Caldwell, the author of *God's Little Acre*, remarked, "I learned early in life that you can be a reader or a writer. I decided to be a writer." Although this comment may help explain his career choice, it masks the reciprocal relationship between these two skills. Reading serves as a source of inspiration for writing and a wellspring for ideas. Writing in turn enhances understanding and extends thinking about what is read (Hidi & Anderson, 1986).

One strategy that benefits both reading and writing is summarization (Dee-Lucas & DiVesta, 1980). The act of writing a summary makes reading material more memorable and preserves important thoughts and ideas for later use. Its value was captured by British author F.L. Lucas, who noted that summarizing serves as a log or photograph of one's voyages with books: "For memory, in most of us, is a liar with galloping consumption."

Learning how to write good summaries may also help students write more precisely. This is no small feat. Some of the our most memorable documents are quite concise. Lincoln's Gettysburg Address is only 266 words long. The Bill of Rights contains 438 words. Lawyers and technical writers would do well to emulate these models. For example, a federal directive designed to regulate the price of cabbage is more than 26,000 words in length.

Writing a good summary involves making the right decisions about what to eliminate as well as what to keep and how to condense it (Brown & Day, 1983). This is a challenging task for many students with learning disabilities. Consider the summary that follows, in which a child tries to provide a succinct description of Wellington's famous victory against the French. The most important information is eliminated, and trivial facts are brewed together to form an unusual synopsis.

> The Duck of Wellington won a big battle and when he finished he had one arm and one eye and he looked through the telescope with his blind eye and said it was alright and that is how he won the battle.

The *summary-writing strategy* presented in this chapter is designed to help students write a clear, concise, and accurate written summary (Nelson, Smith, & Dodd, 1992). This includes identifying the main idea and important information in text, writing an initial summary of this information, and revising it for clarity.

THE SUMMARY-WRITING STRATEGY

The summary-writing strategy involves five basic steps: read the text, identify main ideas and information, plan and organize the summary, write it, and revise it (Nelson et al., 1992).

Step 1. The student reads the text.

Step 2. The student identifies the main idea and the most important information about it. First, the student asks, "What is the main idea?" and writes it down (see Figure 9.1). Second, the child inquires, "What important things did the writer say about the main idea?" Each important thing is written directly under the main idea. Third, the student reexamines the text to ensure that he or she got it right. The main idea and list of important information is revised as needed.

Step 3. The student prepares a plan for writing the summary. First, the child writes a topic sentence for the main idea (see Figure 9.1). Second, the student organizes the information recorded during Step 2 by numbering which item will go first, second, third, fourth, and so on. Third, the student examines the recorded information to determine whether any important ideas are missing or any unimportant information can be eliminated.

Step 4. The student uses the plan to write the summary.

Step 5. The student reads the summary and asks, "Is there anything that is unclear?" A classmate is also asked to do the same thing. Based on the results of these evaluations, the summary is rewritten if necessary.

Rationale

Students with learning disabilities do not typically put into play the processes and resources needed to write a good summary. They do not think carefully or thoroughly about what they plan to write and they do little to improve the quality or clarity of their message (Graham & Harris, 1989b). The summary-writing strategy helps students organize their writing behavior so that they are more reflective, plan more thoughtfully, and expend more effort. This includes analyzing text to identify the most critical informa-

Step 1
Think to yourself: "What was the main idea?"
Write it down.

Step 2
Think to yourself: "What important things did the writer say about the main idea?"
Write down the important things the writer said.

1.

2.

3.

4.

5.

Step 3
Go back and check to make sure you understood what the main idea was and the important things the writer said about this.

Step 4
Think to yourself: "What is the main idea or topic that I am going to write about?"
Write a topic sentence for your summary.

Step 5
Think to yourself: "How should I group my ideas?" Put a "1" next to the idea you want to be first, put a "2" next to the idea that you want to be second, and so on.

Step 6
Think to yourself: "First, is there any important information that I left out, and second, is there any unimportant information that I can take out?"

Step 7
Write a summary about what you read.

Step 8
Read your summary and think to yourself: "Is there anything that is not clear?" Rewrite your summary (if necessary).

Step 9
Ask your classmate to read your summary and ask him or her to tell you if there is anything that is not clear. Rewrite your summary (if necessary).

Writing Better: Effective Strategies for Teaching Students with Learning Difficulties, by S. Graham and K.R. Harris, © 2005 Paul H. Brookes Publishing Co., Inc. All rights reserved.
Figure 9.1. Summary-writing strategy guide. (From Nelson, R., Smith, D., & Dodd, J. [1992]. The effects of teaching a summary skills strategy to students identified as learning disabled on their comprehension of science text. *Education and Treatment of Children, 15,* 228–243; reprinted by permission.)

tion, developing a plan for writing the summary, and revising the resulting summary to make it clearer. The strategy also prompts students to evaluate and modify their performance as they carry out these tasks.

Teaching the Strategy

Students with learning disabilities can be taught to use the summary-writing strategy in five to six 45-minute instructional sessions (Nelson et al., 1992). The procedure is taught in five sessions.

Session 1   In the first session, the strategy is introduced to students. First, the teacher describes a summary: "A summary should contain only important information; personal and unnecessary information is left out. Information is combined when possible. Information is added to make the summary more understandable, and it is written in your own words." Next, cues are identified that help readers determine the main ideas. These include large type, italics, underlined words, repetition of words and sentences, introductory or summary sentences, as well as words or phrases such as "important," "relevant," and "the purpose is." Then, the teacher describes the strategy and the rationale for each step. Students listen and follow along as the teacher models how to use the strategy. Following a discussion of the steps the teacher took to apply the strategy, students restate the definition of a summary, the cues used to find main ideas, the steps of the strategy, and the importance of each step.

Sessions 2–5   The format for the rest of the lessons follows a three-part teaching script: review, modeling, and guided practice. At the start of each session, the steps of the strategy are reviewed. Then the teacher models how to use the strategy while thinking out loud. This includes using self-statements such as "I need to" or "What is it I have to do?" Throughout the process, students are encouraged to help the teacher apply the strategy. After modeling, the teacher and students discuss the importance of thinking to themselves as they write a summary. Finally, students practice as a group using the strategy, receiving guidance from the teacher as needed.

Validation

The summary-writing strategy was validated with fourth- and sixth-grade students with learning disabilities (Nelson et al., 1992). All students had been identified by the participating school district as having a learning disability. School criteria for classifying students as having a learning disability were not provided. The students were culturally diverse, and their percentile ranking on a group-administered test of reading comprehension ranged from 16 to 31.

What to Expect

Learning to use the summary-writing strategy had a positive effect on students' writing and reading skills. Summaries written by the participating fourth- and sixth-grade

> **Tip 1:** Don't assume that students know what a main idea is or even some of the cue words that help identify it. For instance, one child indicated that "Italics are what Italians write in." Use examples to define each of these concepts and ask students to find an example of each one in their reading material.
>
> **Tip 2:** One way to help students better understand the concept of a summary is to encourage them to think of it as a table. The main idea is a table top supported by details as represented by the legs of the table (Baumann, 1984).
>
> **Tip 3:** In addition to providing students with practice applying the *summary-writing strategy* as a group, we recommend that students practice applying it individually, receiving assistance from the teacher as needed. This extra step is necessary for many students with learning disabilities to independently master the strategy.

students with learning disabilities became more complete after instruction. The percentage of critical information students included in their summaries rose from 45% to 98% after they learned to use the strategy. There was also a corresponding increase in their comprehension of science material they summarized. The students doubled the number of comprehension questions they answered correctly after instruction, obtaining an average of 94% correct.

Portability

Although the summary-writing strategy has only been tested with fourth- and sixth-grade students with learning disabilities, we expect that the strategy would be effective with other students of the same age. We base this prediction on two observations. First, the process of writing a summary is a complex process based on the application of a number of rules (e.g., design a topic sentence, delete trivial and redundant information). The summary-writing strategy emphasizes the application of these rules and provides a useful framework for accomplishing this task. Second, other research has demonstrated that similar summarization strategies improved the writing and reading performance of a variety of students in the upper elementary grades, including students who find reading challenging (cf. Baumann, 1984; Bean & Steenwyk, 1984; Berkowitz, 1986; Pressley, 2002).

Extensions

One important aspect of extending the summary-writing strategy is to have students apply it broadly as they are initially learning to use it. Nelson and his colleagues (1992) had students practice using the strategy as they read only science material. Students should be encouraged to apply the strategy (with guided assistance) to other types of expository material as well as to narrative text.

For some types of text, such as material with a problem/solution structure, it may be useful to modify the strategy so that students use this organizational pattern to help them create their summaries. For example, before completing Step 1 of the summary-writing strategy ("What was the main idea?"), students might fill out a graphic organizer with a three-box diagram depicting problem, action, and results (see Armbruster, Anderson, & Ostertag, 1987). With this information in hand, students then construct the main idea.

Steps 1 and 2 of the summary-writing strategy may also be modified so that the linkages between the main idea and important details are made more visible. For example, students could write the main idea in a circle in the center of a page and each supporting detail in a circle around it. The connections between main idea and details (and detail to detail) are made apparent through the use of lines with directional arrows. Of course, teachers need to carefully monitor any new modifications or extensions of the strategy (see Chapter 17).

Before ending this chapter, we would like to share two more child-generated summaries. One involves vitamins, the other locations.

> Lack of vitamin A is not as bad as lack of vitamin B which in turn will not have so many bad effects as will the lack of vitamin C and so on down the alphabet.

> By learning that Krakston is located between Sumatra and Java, I Now know three places I can look for instead of just one.

Writing Strategies that Are Genre Specific

Each genre has its own rules and established conventions. Some aspects of a genre are quite obvious. If you are going to write a ghost story, you must put a ghost in it. Other characteristics are more abstract but no less important. Murder mysteries, for example, contain many of the same basic elements: "A murder occurs; many are suspected; all but one suspect, who is the murderer, are eliminated; the murderer is arrested or dies." With some slight variation, this basic formula described by W.H. Auden captures the essence of the murder mystery genre. When writers ignore a genre's basic elements or building blocks, they run the risk of confusing or even alienating the reader. No one wants to read a mystery that is missing needed clues. As the novelist John Lowery Nixon noted, "You must play fair by giving all the clues, but disguise them by immediately distracting the reader with something else."

Some children, especially those with learning disabilities, are not fully acquainted with the rules and conventions of common writing genres (Graham, Schwartz, & MacArthur, 1993). One child described a fairy tale as "something that never happened a long time ago." A second student indicated that fiction was "a way to make fire." Another pupil defined *fiction* as "those books which are fixed on the shelf and not to be moved."

In this section, we present writing strategies that are designed specifically for a particular genre. This includes validated strategies for creating a story (Chapter 10), expressing an opinion (Chapter 11), providing explanations (Chapter 12), comparing and contrasting (Chapter 13), and developing a report (Chapter 14). With these strategies, students learn how to plan and revise text while also attending to established genre conventions or rules.

As in the previous sections of this book, each strategy is presented along with the rationale for using it with students with learning disabilities. Procedures for teaching the strategy, as well as scientific evidence on its effectiveness, are then described. (As a reminder, an effect size of .20 is considered small, .50 is medium, and .80 is large.) We also consider who else might benefit from learning the strategy and how its use can be extended and modified.

Most of the strategies included in this section are taught using the *self-regulated strategy development* (SRSD) model presented in Chapter 3. For the sake of brevity, we do not repeatedly present this model when describing how to teach these specific strategies. Instead, we refer the reader to Chapter 3, where a full description of SRSD and examples of how to implement it are provided. Instructional issues that are germane to each of these strategies, however, are addressed in each chapter. Finally, the teaching methods for all other strategies are fully described in their respective chapters.

CHAPTER 10

Story Writing

Advice about word choice is quite common and varied. Winston Churchill held, "Short words are best, and the old words when short are best of all." Mark Twain counseled, "When you catch an adjective, kill it." C.S. Lewis recommended, "Don't use words too big for the subject." The underlying theme in all of these suggestions is that good writing is made of the right words. This is true for beginning writers as well. The quality of students' writing is related to their choice of words (Grobe, 1981; Steward & Grobe, 1979).

Some types of words appear more often in one genre than another. For example, action verbs, such as *running* and *playing*, are more likely to appear in stories rather than persuasive essays or other types of expository text. The first story-writing strategy presented in this chapter, *vocabulary*, capitalizes on this observation. With this strategy, students generate action and describing words that can be used in their story. This not only helps them think about the words they plan to use but also stimulates thinking about the content of the story as well.

The second story-writing strategy, *story grammar*, is based on a procedure used by writers such as Isaac Asimov, the creator of the *Foundation* series and *I, Robot*. Before starting to write, he established the structure for a story by delineating some of its basic parts. This included deciding how the story ended and the problem it centered around.

The story grammar strategy employs this same basic approach but extends it to a broader range of story elements. Before writing, students create a structure for their story by establishing characters, setting, problem, actions, reactions, and resolution. These elements help them think about all of the major aspects of their story, providing an initial plan for writing it.

STRATEGY I: THE VOCABULARY STRATEGY

With the vocabulary strategy, students brainstorm action and describing words that can be used in their story (Harris & Graham, 1985). This strategy focuses on action and describing words over other types of vocabulary because stories produced by many students with learning disabilities lack richness and color. The strategy also emphasizes generating possible words instead of ideas. Some children short-circuit the brainstorming process of generating ideas when they become bogged down with thinking about how their ideas are connected (Scardamalia & Bereiter, 1986). The vocabulary strategy consists of the following five steps.

Step 1. Students are first asked to think of a good idea for their story. This is recorded at the top of the planning sheet (see Figure 10.1).

Step 2. Keeping their story idea in mind, students brainstorm action and describing words to include in the story. Action words are recorded on the left side of the planning sheet; describing words are written on the right side.

Step 3. Students then write their story, using some or all of the words generated. The emphasis is on "writing a good story" and using words that "help your story."

Step 4. Once the first draft is completed, students read over the story and identify trouble spots and places where better words can be used.

Step 5. Students revise the trouble spots and make word additions, deletions, or substitutions to enhance the story and their choice of words.

Although the strategy focuses on generating and using good action and describing words, making sense and developing a good story line are emphasized throughout. Without this emphasis, some children will undoubtedly decide that the primary goal is to get as many of these words in the story as possible, forgetting that the main purpose of story writing is to communicate, inform, or entertain.

Vocabulary Strategy for Story Writing

Story idea:

Action words: **Describing words:**

Remember: Write a story that makes sense, and use your action and describing words.

Writing Better: Effective Strategies for Teaching Students with Learning Difficulties, by S. Graham and K.R. Harris,
© 2005 Paul H. Brookes Publishing Co., Inc. All rights reserved.
Figure 10.1. Planning sheet for the vocabulary strategy.

It is also important to note that the first two steps of the vocabulary strategy are not sequential. Instead, they are applied recursively. The selection of a story line influences the words selected, and the words selected provide the writer with additional ideas for developing the story line.

Teaching the Strategy

The general procedures for teaching the vocabulary strategy are described in Chapter 3. Thus, only instructional procedures specific to this strategy are presented here.

Instruction in how to use the vocabulary strategy starts with action words. Once students can successfully apply the strategy with action words, they learn to use it with both action and describing words. Students with learning disabilities, at least at the sixth-grade level, can learn to use the strategy with both types of words in eight to twelve 45-minute sessions.

Some students are not familiar with the terms *action words* and *describing words*. (An action word is an active verb and a describing word is an adjective.) Before students learn to use the strategy, they are taught the meaning of these concepts. This is done by defining action word and describing word and providing examples of each (see Figure 10.2). Students are not taught the strategy until they can independently generate at least three examples of their own for each type of word.

We decided to use informal terms, such as *describing words* for adjectives, because some students with learning disabilities struggle with the traditional labels for parts of speech. One child told us that he had "failed adjectives" in his other class. Another student correctly indicated that "an active verb shows action" but revealed that his understanding was shaky when he went on to say, "a passive verb shows passion."

The teacher introduces the vocabulary strategy by establishing its purpose ("to write better stories that are more colorful and interesting to read") and describing how each step operates using a chart (see Figure 10.3). The teacher emphasizes how the steps are interrelated and how using good action and describing words improves a story.

At this point, students are asked to work collaboratively with the teacher to learn the strategy. They are told that they will first learn to use it with action words. The

---

Action words tell what people, things, or animals do. They are *doing* words.
- He *jumped* and *shouted* at the game.
- The man *worried* and *thought* about her.
- The book *fell* on the floor.

Describing words tell more about people, animals, places, or things. They help to paint a picture. Describing words may tell about color, shape, size, number, feelings, smell, sounds, taste, and so forth.
- The *sick* girl went home.
- There were *five* boxes.
- The *pretty* leaf was *red.*
- I like *salty* popcorn.

Writing Better: Effective Strategies for Teaching Students with Learning Difficulties, by S. Graham and K.R. Harris, © 2005 Paul H. Brookes Publishing Co., Inc. All rights reserved.
Figure 10.2. Chart for action and describing words.

1. Think of a good story idea.

2. Write down good words for my story.

3. Write my story—Use good words and make sure my story makes sense.

4. Read over my story and ask myself—Did I write a good story?

5. Fix my story—Can I use more good words?

Writing Better: Effective Strategies for Teaching Students with Learning Difficulties, by S. Graham and K.R. Harris,
© 2005 Paul H. Brookes Publishing Co., Inc. All rights reserved.
Figure 10.3.   Chart for the vocabulary strategy.

students select a previously written story from their writing folder and count and graph the number of action words included. As they practice using the strategy to write stories, they continue to graph their performance. This provides them with a visual representation of the effectiveness of the strategy.

Next, the teacher models how to apply the strategy, using the planning sheet in Figure 10.1 (the column for describing words is eliminated). While brainstorming action words (Step 2), the teacher uses self-statements such as, "Take my time," "Good words will come to me," and "Let my mind be free." During modeling, students help the teacher apply the strategy and construct a story. This includes helping the teacher think of a story line, generating action words, writing the story, and fixing it. Once the story is completed, students identify what the teacher said that helped to get started, write the story, and evaluate the story. They record examples of statements (in their own words) that they plan to use to help them with these same processes.

Each day before they practice using the strategy, students spend about 5 minutes rehearsing or memorizing the steps of the strategy. As they practice using the strategy (either with the teacher, with another student, or independently), they set a goal for how many action words they plan to include in their story. After the story is completed, they count the number of action words, record their performance on a graph, and note their success in attaining the goal. Once students can independently and effectively use the vocabulary strategy with action words, they learn to apply it with action and describing words together.

What to Expect

The vocabulary strategy was validated with sixth-grade students with learning disabilities. These students' scores on an individually administered intelligence test were in the average range (between 85 and 115), but their achievement in reading was at least 2 years below their grade level placement. Their teacher also indicated that each child had difficulty with writing. This observation was confirmed by the students' scores on an individual test of writing achievement.

Learning to use the vocabulary strategy had a positive impact on three aspects of these students' stories. There was an increase in the number of action and describing words included in their stories. After instruction, action words increased by 200% and

---

Tip 1: Some students need help in setting realistic goals for their papers. One student who typically used three or four action words in a story wanted to set a goal to include "50 action words"! Fortunately, the teacher helped her develop a more appropriate goal.

Tip 2: Some students become so enamored with setting and obtaining goals that the primary purpose—to write a good story—is forgotten. For example, a student may use too many describing words to portray a person, place, or thing. One students included a 12-color rainbow so that he could get in as many describing words as possible! It was necessary to remind this student that words are only useful if they help the story.

Tip 3: Students may use action or describing words incorrectly. For example, one student wrote, "Period costumes are all covered with dots." Whenever this occurs, the teacher needs to discuss the correct meaning of the word with the child.

---

describing words by 357%. Students also wrote longer stories after instruction, increasing their overall output by 152%. Even more important, scores for overall quality of writing more than doubled once they learned to use the strategy.

The impact of the strategy is illustrated in the two stories that follow. The first was written before instruction and the second after the child had learned to use the strategy. Spelling, capitalization, and punctuation miscues were corrected in both stories. The second story is more complete and richer than the first story. It contains more ideas as well as more action and describing words.

Before instruction:

Me and my son are leaving to fly a space shuttle. And some day, me and my son will hopefully fly one. My son says, "When he grows up, he going to fly one." When he finishes school, me and my wife are going to put him through school and let him learn how to fly. And when he starts to fly space ships, he will be able to buy his own house. Now that he's grow up, he will start flying in 3 months, and he said he, "I will love it a lot."

After instruction:

The Dog and His Food

One day, this brown puppy was sitting on the porch, and these boys started throwing rocks at the puppy. And one hit the puppy, and the puppy sadly ran into the house. And the girl quickly came downstairs and said, "I'm going to take the puppy for a walk." So she went and got the long dog leash and took him for a walk. And when he was walking, she tripped and fell hard on a rock and cut her hand and had to get 15 stitches on her hand. When she got home from the doctors, she went looking for the puppy. All day, she looked, and then she saw him. She took him home and gave him a big bath, and after she gave him a bath, she fed him a big bowl of dog food. And she was very happy that she found him.

Portability

The value of the vocabulary strategy for other students is unclear. There have been no scientific tests of its application beyond sixth-grade students with learning disabilities. We expect that the strategy would be effective with other students whose stories contain few ideas or little elaboration because it is designed to stimulate the generation of ideas and direct attention to word selection.

Extensions

One way that the vocabulary strategy can be adapted is by applying it to a similar genre, such as personal narratives. Action and describing words are commonly used when children describe a particular event in their lives.

The strategy can also be modified so that it can be used more widely by having students brainstorm any words that they think might be useful in writing a paper. Figure 10.4 presents a modified version of the strategy that can be applied more broadly to any genre. As with other recommended extensions, teachers need to assess the effectiveness of these adaptations (see Chapter 17).

---

1 Think of a good idea for my paper.

2. Write down good words for my paper.

3. Write my paper—Use good words and make sure my paper makes sense.

4. Read over my paper and ask myself—Did I write a good paper?

5. Fix my paper—Can I use more good words?

Writing Better: Effective Strategies for Teaching Students with Learning Difficulties, by S. Graham and K.R. Harris, © 2005 Paul H. Brookes Publishing Co., Inc. All rights reserved.
Figure 10.4.   Chart for general application of the vocabulary strategy.

STRATEGY 2: THE STORY GRAMMAR STRATEGY

With the story grammar strategy, students generate ideas for each of the basic parts of a story before starting their first draft (Danoff et al., 1993; Graham & Harris, 1989a; Sawyer et al., 1992). These notes provide an initial writing plan that is embellished and upgraded as they write. Students generate notes for characters, locale, time, characters' goals, characters' feelings, and story ending. The strategy consists of the following steps (see also Figures 10.5 and 10.6).

Step 1. Students first think of a good story idea to share with others.

1. Think of a story that I would like to share with others.
2. Let my mind be free.
3. Write down the story part reminder:
   W - W - W
   WHAT = 2
   HOW = 2
4. Make notes of my ideas for each part.
5. Write my story—Use good parts, add, elaborate, or revise as I write or afterward, and make sense.

Figure 10.5. Chart for the story grammar strategy.

Step 2. They use the prompt "Let my mind be free" as they brainstorm ideas for each part of their story. This self-statement reminds them to generate as many ideas as possible and keep the brainstorming process going as long as possible.

Step 3. They write the reminder for story parts at the top of a piece of paper. They then record ideas they brainstorm for each part below the reminder. The reminder is

W - W - W, WHAT = 2, HOW = 2

The Ws stand for:

- *W*ho is the main character; who else is in the story?
- *W*hen does the story take place?
- *W*here does the story take place?

The two WHATs stand for:

- *What* does the main character want to do; what do the other characters want to do?
- *What* happens when the main character tries to do it; what happens with the other characters?

Story Part Reminder

Who is the main character; who else is in the story?
When does the story take place?
Where does the story take place?
What does the main character want to do; what do the other characters want to do?
What happens when the main character tries to do it; what happens with the other characters?
How does the story end?
How does the main character feel; how do other characters feel?

Figure 10.6. Chart for story part reminder questions.

The two HOWs stand for:

- *How* does the story end?
- *How* does the main character feel; how do other characters feel?

Step 4. Students write a story using their notes as a guide.

Step 5. As they write, the emphasis is on "creating a good story." Students are encouraged to add new ideas as well as elaborate and modify their initial thoughts in order to write a story that makes sense and that others will find enjoyable.

Teaching the Strategy

An illustration of how to teach the story grammar strategy is presented in Chapter 3 (see Example 1: Teaching the Story Grammar Strategy). Thus, it is not repeated here. Students with learning disabilities, at least at the fourth- through sixth-grade level, typically require 8–10 hours of instruction to master the strategy.

We would like to note that several minor adaptations of the story grammar strategy have been used successfully with children with learning disabilities. One involves using a software program in which children respond to 11 questions or prompts about their story before starting to write (Bahr, Nelson, & Van Meter, 1996). The first three prompts help students generate a story idea. The next eight prompts replicate and extend the questions included in the story grammar strategy.

- List two or three ideas for a story.
- Choose one of your ideas and type a working title.
- Why did you choose this topic?
- Who or what is the main character or characters?
- Where does the story take place?
- When does the story take place?
- What happens to the main character or characters?
- What does the main character or characters do?
- Why does the main character or characters do that?
- How does the main character or characters feel?
- How will your story end?

Another small adaptation involves using a different mnemonic for the story parts or elements. Instead of the mnemonic W − W − W, WHAT = 2, HOW = 2, the acronym SPACE is used (Graham & Harris, 1989c; MacArthur, Graham, Schwartz, & Schafer, 1995). The letters of this acronym stand for *S*etting (who, when, where); *P*urpose (what the main character or characters want to do); *A*ction (what the main character or characters do); *C*onclusion (how the story ends); and *E*motions (how the main character or characters feel).

Zipprich (1995) developed a slightly different procedure for generating planning notes (Steps 3 and 4 of the story grammar strategy). Students brainstorm ideas for the title, setting, problem (including goal), action, and outcome using a story web. Her planning sheet is presented in Figure 10.7.

Finally, in our most recent work with struggling writers in the second and third grades, we culled the five steps of the story grammar strategy (see Figure 10.5) down to

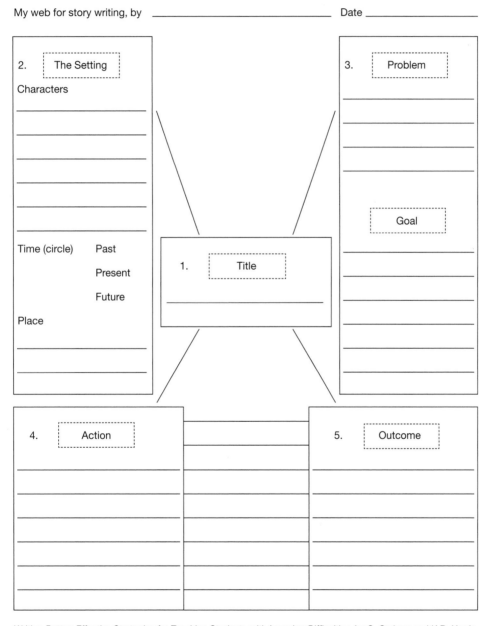

My web for story writing, by _____ Date _____

Writing Better: Effective Strategies for Teaching Students with Learning Difficulties, by S. Graham and K.R. Harris, © 2005 Paul H. Brookes Publishing Co., Inc. All rights reserved.
Figure 10.7.   Story grammar planning sheet.

Tip 1: When a father commented on how poorly his child made her bed, the child shot back, "It's just a rough draft." This bit of witticism can also be applied to the story grammar strategy. Some children want to write their notes as full sentences and then complain when they write them again as part of their story. Ideas for each story grammar part should be recorded as notes.

Tip 2: The difficulty that some children experience getting ideas for writing is reflected in this commentary on Dante: "Dante was a writer. He got permission to go to Hell, and when he returned, he wrote about his experiences." Fortunately, not every one can go to Hell to get ideas. If students experience difficulty brainstorming ideas, pair them with another child during planning or brainstorm ideas as a class before writing a first draft.

Tip 3: A child from an upwardly mobile family wrote the following story: "Once upon a time, there was a poor family. The father was poor. The mother was poor. The children were poor. The nannies were poor. The pool man was poor. The personal trainer was poor." In addition to being repetitious, the story is not believable. Before children share their stories with the class, provide them with feedback aimed at helping them avoid such pitfalls.

three steps (Graham, Harris, & Mason, in press; Harris, Graham, & Mason, 2004). The acronym POW is used to help students remember the following three steps for planning and writing a story:

- *Pick* my idea.

- *Organize* my notes.

- *Write* and say more.

With *Pick my idea*, students think of a good story to share with others. *Organize my notes* involves writing down the story part reminder and generating notes for each part. *Write and say more* prompts students to continue the process of planning while writing.

What to Expect

The story grammar strategy was validated in two separate studies. In the first study (Sawyer et al., 1992), small groups of fifth- and sixth-grade students with learning disabilities were taught to use the strategy. These students' scores on an individually administered intelligence test ranged from 80 to 120 (mean IQ score = 94). Their reading and writing scores were 2 or more years below grade level, and teachers indicated that each student experienced difficulty with writing.

The effects of the story grammar strategy on the story writing performance of these students were very strong (Sawyer et al., 1992). In comparison to children who practiced writing stories, students who learned the strategy developed more fully crafted papers, which included most if not all of the basic elements of a story (effect size = 3.52). Their stories were also qualitatively better (effect size = 1.47).

In the second study (Danoff et al., 1993), fourth- and fifth-grade students with learning disabilities were taught to use the story grammar strategy. These children were in an inclusive classroom, involving a co-teaching arrangement with a special education teacher and a general classroom teacher. The students' scores on an individually administered intelligence test ranged from 89 to 105. Performance on an individually administered reading test was 1–2 *SD* below the mean of the normative sample. Teachers also indicated that each student had difficulty with writing.

After instruction, these students included twice as many elements in their stories as they did during baseline (Danoff et al., 1993). The length of their stories doubled as well, and scores for story quality rose by 136%.

The impact of the story grammar strategy is illustrated in the two stories that follow. The first was written before instruction started and the second after instruction ended. Spelling, capitalization, and punctuation miscues were corrected in both papers. The first story is basically a description, whereas the second story is complete with an unusual twist at the end.

Before instruction:

One day, I was running in the field. It was very hot and leaves was falling. There are lots of hills and nice green grass. There are huge trees that are full of leaves. There were lots of flowers in the garden. It was a bit of shade. Lots of bushes that has leaves on it. And the summer was nice.

After instruction:

Once upon a time, an Indian named Rob wanted to ride a horse again. The reason why Rob wanted to ride again is because 2 years ago, he had an accident on the horse. Rob had got hurt bad. He had to get his legs cut off. So one day Rob went outside in his wheelchair and he seen a horse. It was all white and then Rob wheeled his chair over to the horse. And Rob grabbed the horse and pulled his self up. Rob was on the horse. Then the horse took off. And the horse was kicking and then he jumped up and Rob, the brave Indian, fell off and died. He was brave, so that is the end of him.

Portability

The story grammar strategy is quite portable. It is not only an effective writing strategy for students with learning disabilities in grades 4–6, but it also can improve the writing performance of average writers in the upper elementary grades (Danoff et al., 1993) as well as struggling writers in grades 2 and 3 (Graham et al., 2004; Harris et al., 2004; Saddler, Moran, Graham, & Harris, 2004). When tested with younger writers, it was effective with poor writers with and without disabilities, including children with speech and language difficulties, learning disabilities, attention-deficit/hyperactivity disorders, behavioral difficulties, and developmental delays.

Extensions

Beal, Garrod, and Bonitatibus (1993) demonstrated one way to extend the story grammar strategy. Instead of having students generate notes for each story part, they asked third-grade children who were poor writers to use the questions below to find the parts of their story that were unclear and correct them. This revising strategy improved the communicative quality of students' text.

- Who are the people in the story and what are they like?
- What is happening in the story?
- Why are they doing what they did?
- Where does the story take place?
- When does the story take place?

Although the story grammar strategy is designed to increase the level of detail in a story, some teachers have modified the strategy by adding a specific prompt to generate even more detail for each story part. For example, one teacher in Washington, D.C., modified the mnemonic SPACE to SPACED. The last letter reminded students to add *detail* for each story part.

Teachers can further increase attention to detail by providing more guidance on the types of information students should think about for each story part. For example, Leavell and Ioannides (1993) helped children further develop their story characters by asking them to describe their physical appearance, speech and actions, and thoughts and emotions. The effectiveness of each of these extensions needs to be tested using procedures described in Chapter 17.

CHAPTER II

Persuasive Writing

Mark Twain was not shy about expressing his opinions or lampooning other people's views. After hearing several scholars argue about who wrote the plays and sonnets attributed to Shakespeare, he exclaimed,

> It wasn't William Shakespeare who really wrote those plays, but another Englishman who was born on the same day at the same hour as he, and who died on the same day, and to carry the coincidences still further, was also named William Shakespeare.

This argument did not fade away with the passing of one of America's greatest humorists, but it found new life in a child who declared that Shakespeare's material was written by "William Shakespeare, the Different, another man by the same name."

Just like this youngster, children are frequently asked to take a position on some topic and defend it in writing. The power of this defense depends in large part on the quality of the evidence they offer to support their premise. As the two examples that follow illustrate, some students, including those with learning disabilities, are not particularly adept at developing a convincing argument.

> Mad dogs must be shot as we have no way of telling who they are mad at and might bite.

> One benefit of taking Latin is that you may come across someone who's been in a car crash, and they're trapped in the car, and all they can speak is Latin, and you couldn't help them because you couldn't understand them.

In addition to providing weak evidence to support their claim, students with learning disabilities may not include all of the basic parts of an argument. They often fail to let the reader know their position, refute evidence for the other side, or provide a concluding statement (De La Paz & Graham, 1997; Graham, 1990). The first two strategies presented in this chapter, *three-step strategy with TREE* and *STOP and DARE*, are designed to help students think through their argument before writing it. Both strategies direct students' thinking by focusing their attention on the basic parts of an essay as well as the quality of the evidence. The third strategy, *SCAN*, provides a step-by-step procedure for revising the substance and mechanics of opinion essays.

STRATEGY I: THE THREE-STEP STRATEGY WITH TREE

The three-step strategy with TREE provides a general framework for planning and writing a simple persuasive essay (Graham & Harris, 1989c; Sexton et al., 1998). This includes identifying the audience, setting a purpose, planning the paper, and upgrading or modifying the plan while writing. A prominent feature of the strategy is the use of genre-specific prompts for generating, organizing, and evaluating possible writing content. These prompts focus on developing a clear and concise premise, supporting reasons, and a summary statement. The steps of the strategy are described below.

Step 1. Students first identify their audience and the goal for writing the paper (see Figure 11.1). They ask themselves two questions:

- Who will read my paper?

- Why am I writing this paper?

Step 2. Students develop a plan, using a series of genre-specific prompts (or a structural frame) designed to help them generate, evaluate, and organize possible writing content for their argument. To guide this process, students plan what to say using TREE. TREE is a mnemonic that reminds students to generate or brainstorm notes for each part of a simple persuasive essay: a premise or topic sentence (states what you believe), supporting reasons, and summary statement or ending. The mnemonic also prompts students to evaluate the viability of each of the possible reasons they generate. TREE reminds students to carry out these four activities:

- Note *t*opic sentence.

- Note *r*easons.

- *E*xamine reasons—Will my reader believe this?

- Note *e*nding.

When brainstorming possible reasons, students are asked to suspend or hold their judgment on the value of each idea. Once they have completed this process, they "examine each reason," crossing out any item that readers might see as weak or unacceptable. If they think of other ideas at this point, they add the new ideas to their list and evaluate

Step 1.	**Think.**
	Who will read my paper? _____
	Why am I writing this paper? _____
Step 2.	**Plan what to say using TREE.**
	Note **t**opic sentence: _____
	Note **r**easons:
	Examine each reason above—Will my reader believe this?
	Note **e**nding: _____
	Number which idea will go first, second, third, and so on.
Step 3.	**Write and say more.**

Figure 11.1. Planning sheet for three-step strategy with TREE.

each in turn. When they are done generating and evaluating these notes, they organize the notes by numbering which idea they plan to introduce first, second, third, and so forth.

Step 3. Using their plan as a guide, students write their papers and continue the process of planning while writing. As a reminder, students tell themselves to *Write and say more*.

Teaching the Strategy

An illustration of how to teach the three-step strategy with TREE was presented in Chapter 3 (see Example 2: Teaching the Three-Step Strategy with TREE). Consequently, it is not repeated here. Students with learning disabilities, at least at the fifth- and sixth-grade level, typically require 6–8 hours of instruction to master the strategy.

In recent studies (Graham, Harris, & Mason, in press; Harris, Graham, & Mason, 2004), we made one minor adaptation to the mnemonic TREE. This modification involves the prompt "*Examine reasons—Will my reader buy this?*" This directive was replaced by "*Note examples,*" asking students to generate examples for each of their reasons. This change in prompts placed more emphasis on providing additional elaboration for each supporting reason. Students are still encouraged to examine the veracity of their supporting reasons. However, they are not provided with a prompt to do so. For students who need such a prompt, the mnemonic TREE can be changed to TREED, with the D reminding them to "Add *d*etails."

What to Expect

The three-step strategy with TREE was validated in two separate studies. In the first study (Graham & Harris, 1989c), sixth-grade students with learning disabilities were taught to use the strategy. These students' scores on individually administered intelligence tests ranged from 89 to 101. Their scores on a norm-referenced writing measure were at or below the 25th percentile. Reading scores were 2 or more years below grade level.

Learning to use the three-step strategy with TREE had a positive impact on these sixth-grade students' persuasive writing (Graham & Harris, 1989c). Students' scores for overall quality doubled following instruction, as did their inclusion of the basic structural elements of an argument. Prior to instruction, only 7% of the essays written by students included a premise, supporting reasons, and a summary statement. This increased to 82% following instruction. There was a modest increase in essay length (131%).

The fifth- and sixth-grade students with learning disabilities in the second study (Sexton et al., 1998) attended a school that employed an inclusive model for special education services. These students' scores on an individually administered intelligence test ranged from 81 to 117. Their reading scores were 2 or more years below grade level. With the exception of one child, students' scores on a norm-referenced writing measure were at or below the 16th percentile. According to their teacher, however, all of the students had difficulty with writing. Students also displayed a low level of motivation for writing.

The second study (Sexton et al., 1998) replicated the findings from the first investigation (Graham & Harris, 1989c). Following instruction, scores for overall quality as well as inclusion of basic structural elements more than doubled. Length of essays increased by 181%.

The impact of the three-step strategy with TREE is illustrated in the two essays below. The first was written before instruction and the second after. Spelling, capitalization, and punctuation miscues have been corrected in both papers.

Before instruction:

No, because we went to for 180 and we need to have fun in the summer, and rest our brains before we start school again.

After instruction:

I think school rules are necessary. If there were no rules, people would be doing whatever they want. Not listening to the teacher and eating gum, and screaming, and jumping on furniture. That is why we have rules. So the kids can obey them and we will have a nice school. So that is why I think rules are necessary.

Tip 1: When writing a paper about rubber, a child indicated that "it was necessary to find a substitute. After all, rubber does not grow on trees." Students sometimes have difficulty determining if their supporting ideas are correct or even believable. One way to address this problem is by having a peer give the student feedback on the veracity of the supporting ideas generated with TREE.

Tip 2: Some students want to record their planning ideas as full sentences, converting the eventual writing task into a process of simply recopying their notes word for word. These students need to be reminded that a plan is a sketch of what you intend to do, not the completed project.

Tip 3: When teaching the three-step strategy with TREE to younger students, it may first be necessary to teach them how to brainstorm, paying special attention to the concept of generating ideas without evaluating them at the same time.

Can you identify the writer's premise in the first essay? It was that children should not have to go to school year round. With the second essay, the author makes the premise perfectly clear and provides a more complete and convincing argument.

Portability

The three-step strategy with TREE not only is effective with fifth- and sixth-grade students with learning disabilities but can also improve the writing of younger students. When second- and third-grade children who were struggling with writing were taught the strategy, their persuasive essays became longer, more complete, and qualitatively better (Graham et al., in press; Harris et al., 2004). These beneficial effects occurred for students with and without disabilities, including children with speech and language difficulties, learning disabilities, attention-deficit/hyperactivity disorder, behavioral difficulties, and developmental delays.

Extensions

In our most recent work with struggling writers in second and third grade, we changed the first two steps of the three-step strategy with TREE (Graham et al., in press; Harris et al., 2004). Step 1 became "*P*ick my idea," and it served as a reminder to pick a topic and premise. Step 2 changed to "*O*rganize my notes." This reminded students to generate ideas for each part of the essay using TREE and to sequence them by numbering which idea they planned to use first, second, third, and so forth. Step 3, "*W*rite and say more," stayed the same. The acronym POW was developed to help students remember the three steps:

- *P*ick my idea
- *O*rganize my notes (with TREE)
- *W*rite and say more

POW has also been used as an organizing structure for writing stories (see Chapter 10).

STRATEGY 2: STOP AND DARE

The following is a composition submitted by a precocious 10-year-old child for a newspaper contest in which contributors were asked to imitate "deep thoughts." It deserves a full reading.

> I gaze at the brilliant full moon. The same one, I think to myself, at which Socrates, Aristotle, and Plato gazed. Suddenly, I imagine they appear beside me. I tell Socrates about the national debate over one's right to die and wonder at the constancy of the human condition. I tell Plato that I live in a country that has come the closest to Utopia, and I show him a copy of the U.S. Constitution. I tell Aristotle that we have found many more than four basic elements, and I show him a periodic table. I get a box of kitchen matches and strike one. They gasp with wonder. We spend the rest of the night lighting farts.

The idea of encouraging deep thought is especially important when writing a persuasive essay. The writer should carefully consider both sides of the argument, decide which side to support, and build an argument that is both compelling and fair. The STOP and DARE strategy is designed to help students do just this.

The STOP and DARE strategy provides a general framework for planning and writing a persuasive essay that addresses both sides of an issue (De La Paz & Graham, 1997a, 1997b). In essence, it upgrades TREE by encouraging a more balanced reflection about the topic. The word *STOP* serves as a general reminder to stop, reflect, and plan before writing, and each letter acts as a prompt to carry out a specific activity. The letters remind students to

- *S*uspend judgment
- *T*ake a side
- *O*rganize ideas
- *P*lan more as you write

The purpose of the first step, *suspend judgment*, is to encourage students to consider each side of an argument before taking a position. Students record their thoughts about each side of the topic on the planning sheet (see Figure 11.2). They write their ideas for one side of the argument in the space to the left, and their ideas for the other side in the space to the right. To help them generate ideas, students also consult the following three reminders, which can be written on cue cards:

- Did I list ideas for each side?
- Can I think of anything else? Try to write more.
- Another point I haven't considered yet is . . .

Write topic:

STOP

Suspend judgment. Brainstorm ideas for and against the topic.

For	Against

Take a side. Decide which side you are going to take: For or Against. If you are going to take the "for" side, circle this word; if you are going to take the side "against," circle this word.

Organize ideas. Place a star next to the ideas you plan to use and those you plan to refute.

Plan more as you write. Remember to use **DARE** to see if you used all four parts.

Writing Better: Effective Strategies for Teaching Students with Learning Difficulties, by S. Graham and K.R. Harris,
Figure 11.2.   Planning sheet for STOP and DARE.

During the second step, *Take a side,* students read back through their ideas and decide which position they support or which side has the best support (based on their ideas). They record their decision on the planning sheet by writing "For" above the listed items that support their choice and "Against" above the listed items supporting the other side (see Figure 11.2).

With the third step, *Organize ideas,* students select the ideas on the "for" side that best support their position by placing a star next to each one. They also place a star next to the ideas on the "against" side that they plan to refute. They then number the order in which they plan to present the starred items in their paper. To help them complete these processes, they consult the following cue cards:

- Put a star next to ideas you want to use.

- Put a star next to ideas you want to dispute.

- Number your ideas in the order you will use them.

Students are encouraged to star at least three ideas to support their premise and to refute at least two ideas on the other side. These goals can be adjusted upward, however, as students become more skilled in writing argumentative essays.

The final step, *Plan more as you write*, is a reminder to use the plan already developed and to continue the process of planning while writing. To ensure that they write a complete essay, students check to see that they

- *D*evelop a topic sentence

- *A*dd supporting ideas

- *R*eject arguments for the other side

- *E*nd with a conclusion

The mnemonic DARE is used to remind students of these four parts, and the items are written on a cue card that students consult either while they are writing or once they are done.

Teaching the Strategy

The general procedures used to teach the STOP and DARE strategy are described in Chapter 16. Consequently, only instructional procedures specific to this strategy are presented here.

Before students learn to use the strategy, they need to become familiar with the four parts of an essay embodied in the DARE mnemonic (topic sentence, supporting ideas, rejecting counterarguments, and conclusion). This is done by examining persuasive essays that contain each of these elements. The teacher first defines each element, and then the teacher and students locate them in sample essays until students can do this without teacher help. Teachers should check students' understanding by giving them a topic and asking them to generate ideas for each of the four elements.

It is also important to establish the characteristics of a good persuasive essay before introducing the strategy. This is done by examining essays that differ in quality of presentation and strength of argument. Attention should be directed at the inclusion of the four parts embodied in DARE, the believability and power of the reasons that support the author's premise, and the writer's skill in addressing and refuting counterarguments.

Finally, the planning sheet (see Figure 11.2) and cue cards need to be faded as students become more adept at applying the strategy. To make the strategy as portable as possible, students need to learn to make their own planning sheet on regular notebook paper.

Tip 1: When Bill Cosby asked a young child who Betsy Ross was, she replied "A super model who helped to end slavery." Another child told him that Betsy Ross lived in Philadelphia down "on Brainbridge [Street], near the 7-Eleven." Some children may not be especially knowledgeable or have clear ideas about an assigned topic or issue. One way to address this problem is to have the class generate and discuss their thoughts about both sides of the topic before writing about it.

Tip 2: Another way of helping students to think more deeply about an assigned issue before writing about it is to hold a class debate. Students are assigned to a "pro" or "con" group, and after meeting with their group to develop their argument, they debate the topic. The group that presents the best argument is the winner.

Tip 3: When using DARE, students should be encouraged not only to check to see if they included all four parts of an argument (topic sentence, supporting ideas, rejecting counterarguments, and conclusion) in their paper but also to set a goal to do so before they start to write.

What to Expect

The impact of STOP and DARE on the writing of students with learning disabilities was evaluated in two separate studies. Although all of the students in the first investigation (De La Paz & Graham, 1997a) received services for learning disabilities, they were a heterogeneous group. Their IQ scores ranged from 64 to 128, whereas their reading skills extended from average to 3 years below grade level. All of the students' scores on a norm-referenced writing measure, however, were at or below the 16th percentile. Teachers also confirmed that each child experienced difficulties learning to write.

Learning to use STOP and DARE had a positive impact on these students' persuasive writing (De La Paz & Graham, 1997a). Scores for overall quality doubled after instruction, and similar increases occurred for length and inclusion of basic persuasive essay elements. Before instruction, none of the essays written by students included all of the following elements: a premise, supporting reasons, refutation of counter reasons, and a summary statement. This increased to 70% once instruction ended.

The majority of students in the second study (De La Paz & Graham, 1997b) were in fifth and sixth grade. (About 38% of the youngsters were seventh graders.) These students' scores on an individually administered intelligence test ranged from 80 to 126, with an average of 100. Students' teachers indicated that each child experienced difficulty with writing. These observations were confirmed with a norm-referenced writing test, with all students' scores at or below the 16th percentile. Each child, however, could write a minimum of three connected sentences when composing.

In this study (De La Paz, 1997b), the impact of STOP and DARE on two different modes of writing, dictation and writing by hand, was examined. When students learned to use STOP and DARE while dictating their compositions, the impact was very strong. In comparison with students who learned about the components of good essays and practiced writing and revising them, strategy-instructed students produced longer (effect size = 5.18), more complete (effect size = 3.74), and higher quality essays (effect size = 1.43). The impact of the strategy was more moderate when students learned to use it while writing by hand, as effect sizes for length, completeness, and quality were .32, .55, and .48, respectively.

The impact of STOP and DARE is illustrated in the two essays below. The first paper was written before instruction and the second once instruction had ended. Spelling, capitalization, and punctuation miscues were corrected in both papers.

Before instruction:

I don't think students should go to school in the summer because it is too hot and heat rises. So kids on the top floor would get too hot and sick.

After instruction:

I don't think kids should be able to choose their own food. Some kids were taught to eat right, but most were not. Most kids would eat all junk food. Some kids would copy their parents' eating habits. On the other hand, some would not. Some kids think Made With Real Fruit Juice means that it is good for you, and that is not true. Most kids would take advantage of the situation. You would be unhealthy and have high blood pressure. Thus, I think that parents should choose kid's meals.

Portability

The effectiveness of STOP and DARE has only been tested with fifth-, sixth-, and seventh-grade students with learning disabilities. We expect that the strategy would be effective with other upper-elementary students whose written arguments are one sided or incomplete or contain little elaboration. The strategy is designed to address each of these issues. We do not recommend that the strategy be used with younger children because they may find it more difficult to carefully consider both sides of an argument.

Extensions

One way of extending STOP and DARE is to make it part of a more generalized writing structure, such as POW. This involves some small modifications in both STOP and DARE and POW (see Figure 11.3). The last step of STOP is changed to *Put my plan into play*, reminding students to use the outline they developed during *Organize ideas*. In addition, the last step of POW is changed to *Write, say more, and DARE*. This reminds them to include all four parts in their essay.

Another way to extend STOP and DARE is to eliminate DARE and substitute a checklist for an even more sophisticated argumentative essay (Figure 11.4). Teachers should monitor the effectiveness of both the extensions presented here (see Chapter 17).

Pick my idea	
Organize my notes with	**S**uspend judgment
	Take a side
	Organize ideas
	Put my plan in play
Write, say more, and	**D**evelop a topic sentence
	Add supporting ideas
	Reject arguments for the other side
	End with a conclusion

Writing Better: Effective Strategies for Teaching Students with Learning Difficulties, by S. Graham and K.R. Harris, © 2005 Paul H. Brookes Publishing Co., Inc. All rights reserved.
Figure 11.3.   Chart for integrating STOP and DARE into POW.

_____	Introduction to the problem
_____	Premise
_____	Reasons to support the premise
_____	Counter position
_____	Reasons not to support the counter position
_____	Conclusion

Writing Better: Effective Strategies for Teaching Students with Learning Difficulties, by S. Graham and K.R. Harris, © 2005 Paul H. Brookes Publishing Co., Inc. All rights reserved.
Figure 11.4.   Extension to STOP and DARE: Checklist for more sophisticated persuasive essay.

STRATEGY 3: SCAN

Writing miscues can be quite embarrassing. Consider the following:

- Not responsible for tiepografical errors.

- Lost: small apricot poodle. Reward. Neutered. Like one of the family.

- This is the best book I never read.

- I would like to become a veterinarian. I have had some experience with animals. I have volunteered in dog kennels and cat houses.

These mistakes are minor embarrassments compared with the editorial error committed by a computer programmer working on the Mariner I space probe. A missing comma caused the probe to veer off its course for Venus, costing the U.S. government $18.5 million (Hendrickson, 1994). Fortunately, students' writing miscues and mishaps are rarely this embarrassing or costly. They can, however, lessen the power of an argument. The SCAN revising strategy helps students improve both the substance and form of their argumentative essays.

The SCAN strategy encourages students to examine the clarity and cohesiveness of their papers, add material where necessary, and eliminate mechanical miscues. The steps are presented below and summarized in Figure 11.5.

1. Read the first draft of your essay.

2. Find the sentence that tells what you believe. Is it clear?

3. Add two more reasons why you believe it.

4. **SCAN** each sentence and ask:

   Does it make **sense**?

   Is it **connected** to my belief?

   Can I **add** more?

   Note errors.

5. Make changes.

Figure 11.5.   Steps for the SCAN strategy.

Step 1. The aim of the first step, *Read the first draft of your essay*, is to reacquaint students with the substance of the paper. We recommend that students set the paper aside for at least a day before revising it so they can take a somewhat fresh look at it.

Step 2. The second step—*Find the sentence that tells what you believe. Is it clear?*—encourages students to reexamine the sentence that presents the paper's premise to ensure that it is clear and accurately reflects their belief. If it does not, they revise it.

Step 3. With the third step, *Add two more reasons why you believe it*, students are asked to add at least two more reasons to support the premise. This step may not be necessary for students who already provide strong support for their premise when writing the first draft.

Step 4. The fourth step, *SCAN each sentence*, is the heart and namesake of the strategy. With the exception of the topic sentence, which is examined in Step 2, each sentence is scanned for the following: 1) does it make *sense*—will the reader understand it? 2) is it *connected* to my belief—does it directly support the development of the argument? 3) can I *add* more—do more details need to be added to make the sentence better? and 4) *note* errors—are there any mechanical errors that need to be corrected? More specifically, students are directed to correct any spelling, capitalization, or punctuation errors.

Step 5. As students check the clarity of the topic sentence, add reasons, and scan sentences, they make changes to their papers. This is easier to do if the first draft is double or triple spaced.

Tip 1: "I have read . . . the moon is too hot to live on. Others say it is too cold. So I bet it's just right." While this child's assessment is quite fanciful, it does have a nice sense of balance. Balance is also important with SCAN. One student we worked with stopped correcting mechanical errors once she learned how to use the strategy. We held a short discussion with her, explaining that we were pleased that she was making more substantive changes but that she needed to continue to correct spelling, capitalization, and punctuation errors as well. After this short pep talk, she took a more balanced approach to revising.

Tip 2: A friend's child told us that he knew how to spell his name, and promptly proceeded to do so: "B-i-l-l-y-enter." Obviously, this kid spends a lot of time on the computer. Revising strategies such as SCAN are much easier to use if students do their composing at the computer. This makes it much easier to add, rewrite, delete, and move text.

Tip 3: Step 3, *Add two more reasons why you believe it,* can be expanded to include *Refute two or more reasons for the other side of the argument.*

Teaching the Strategy

General procedures for teaching the SCAN strategy are outlined in Chapter 3. As a result, only procedures specific to teaching this strategy are detailed here.

Before learning to use the strategy, students need to know the basic parts of a persuasive essay (e.g., premise of belief, supporting reasons, and conclusion), including how to define, identify, and generate each part. This is desirable for two reasons. First, successful use of SCAN is dependent on knowing these parts. For example, students must know what a reason is in order to add two or more of them to their paper (Step 3). Second, this knowledge should help students generate and organize writing content for their first draft, resulting in a richer paper to which to apply the strategy.

As students learn to use the strategy, teachers need to pay special attention to helping them detect and correct problems in text. When teachers model the strategy, for example, the processes for locating text problems need to be made visible: "As I say this sentence out loud, something doesn't sound right" or "The reader will need more information to know what I meant here." Teachers and students also need to articulate how each problem can be fixed. Finally, students need to receive feedback on the quality of their revisions and help from a teacher when they are unable to locate a serious text problem and correct it.

What to Expect

The SCAN strategy was validated with fifth- and sixth-grade students with learning disabilities (Graham & MacArthur, 1988). Their IQ scores ranged from 84 to 124. Each child's reading skills were 2 or more years below grade level. Although their teacher indi-

> 1. Read the first draft of your essay.
>
> 2. **SCAN** each sentence:
>
>   Does it make **s**ense?
>
>   Is it **c**onnected to my central idea?
>
>   Can I **a**dd more?
>
>   **N**ote errors.
>
> 3. Make changes.

Writing Better: Effective Strategies for Teaching Students with Learning Difficulties, by S. Graham and K.R. Harris,
© 2005 Paul H. Brookes Publishing Co., Inc. All rights reserved.
Figure 11.6.   The revised and more generic SCAN strategy.

cated that all of these students had difficulty with writing, their scores on a norm-referenced writing measure ranged from average to below average.

Learning to use SCAN had a positive impact on the persuasive essays written by these students (Graham & MacArthur, 1988). The number of revisions that students made after strategy instruction increased threefold. More important, there was a six-fold increase in number of meaning-changing revisions. Before instruction, only 24% of students' revisions focused on substance. Once students learned to use the strategy, however, almost 60% of their revisions involved meaning-changing revisions. These changes in revising had a positive impact on the quality of students' arguments because revised papers were judged to be more persuasive than first drafts. There was also a small increase (about 120%) in the length of students' papers.

Portability

The effectiveness of SCAN has only been tested with fifth- and sixth-grade students with learning disabilities. It may also be effective with other students who do little revising, focus their revising efforts on form and mechanics, or provide little support for their premise. The strategy is designed to address each of these issues.

Extensions

The biggest drawback to the SCAN strategy is that it is genre specific. It can be modified, however, so that it can be used with other writing tasks. This can be done by eliminating the second and third steps and changing a single step in the SCAN mnemonic: "Is it *c*onnected to my belief?" to "Is it *c*onnected to my central idea?" The revised strategy is presented in Figure 11.6. (Teachers should assess the effectiveness of these modifications using procedures contained in Chapter 17.)

CHAPTER 12

Writing Explanations

Writers often have to explain how things work. Mark Twain was a master at this. When explaining how to do research, he advised, "Get your facts first, and then you can distort 'em as much as you please." When speculating why *Huckleberry Finn* was banned in Omaha, he exclaimed,

> I should be sorry to think it was the publishers themselves that got up to this entire little flutter to enable them to unload a book that was taking up too much room in their cellars, but you can never tell what a publisher will do. I have been one myself.

Like Mark Twain's speculation, struggling writers' explanations can sometimes be amusing, even if they are not accurate. Consider the following explanations on first aid, health, and safety:

> To stop a nosebleed, stand on your head till your heart stops beating.

> One important health rule is to take a bath every day. I thought about it all last week.

> To rescue a person who has broken through the ice, take 2 or 3 handkerchiefs and tie them together and then take and shove a boy out to the hole. Throw the boy in the ice with the handkerchiefs and pull them out.

How can we help students with learning disabilities provide more accurate explanations? Rudyard Kipling, in a verse from a poem following "The Elephant's Child" in the *Just-So Stories*, identifies some critical ingredients:

I keep six honest serving-men
(They taught me all I knew);
Their names are What and Why and When
And How and Where and Who.

The first step is to catalog each step or element involved in the process or event being explained by calling upon Kipling's "honest serving-men." This information is then organized so that it provides a full and logical account. The resulting written explanation is then analyzed by the writer (and possibly others) to be sure that it is clear, accurate, and complete.

THE POWER STRATEGY FOR WRITING EXPLANATIONS

The *POWER explanation strategy* provides a structural framework for carrying out the thinking and organizational processes involved in each phase of writing (Englert, Raphael, & Anderson, 1992; Englert, Raphael, Anderson, Anthony, & Stevens, 1991; Raphael, Englert, & Kirschner, 1989). POWER is a mnemonic that identifies five distinct writing phases: Plan, Organize, Write, Edit, and Revise. Thinking and organizational strategies in each of these phases are prompted through the use of *think-sheets* that remind students to carry out these processes. Each think-sheet contains a series of questions that guide students through each phase of writing, as they compose an explanation. The POWER steps for writing an explanation are described below.

Step 1. Plan: The first step is to develop a plan for writing the explanation paper. This includes identifying the topic ("taking care of a kitten"), who will read it ("people who want to have a kitten"), establishing a purpose for writing it ("so people will know how to care for a kitten"), brainstorming ideas for explaining the topic, and grouping these ideas into relevant categories (e.g., food, food care, equipment). The think-sheet for this step is presented in Figure 12.1.

Step 2. Organize: The second step involves developing a text structure map that categorizes and orders students' ideas (see Figure 12.2). Students first identify what is being explained, needed materials (e.g., litter, food, scratch board), and the setting ("house and where to put things"). Next, students organize the explanation by deciding what will come first, second, third, next, and last.

Step 3. Write: With the third step, students use the text structure map (see Figure 12.2) as a guide for writing a first draft of the explanation. Students are encouraged to flesh out the map by adding an introduction, conclusion, details, dialogue, key words, personal examples, and so forth. The think-sheet for this step is a blank sheet of lined colored paper, instead of white, to remind students that this is not the final draft.

Step 4. Edit: The fourth step involves peer editing. Using the think-sheet in Figure 12.3 as a guide, the writer reflects on the first draft, identifying favorite parts, parts that need work, and questions to discuss with the peer editor. At the same

Name: _____ Date: _____

Topic: _____

Who: Who am I writing for? _____

Why: Why am I writing this? _____

What: What do I already know? (Brainstorm)

1. _____

2. _____

3. _____

4. _____

5. _____

6. _____

7. _____

8. _____

How: How do I group my ideas?

Figure 12.1. Planning think-sheet: Explanation paper. (*Source:* Englert, Raphael, Anderson, Anthony, & Stevens [1991].)

time, the peer editor uses the think-sheet in Figure 12.4 to identify strengths and weaknesses. Both students place stars next to the parts they liked best and question marks by the parts that are confusing. They then meet to discuss the paper and how to improve it.

Step 5. Revise: With the aid of a revision think-sheet (see Figure 12.5), students consider how best to revise the paper. They list the editing suggestions generated and received during Step 4 and decide which revisions to implement. A star is placed next to each suggestion that will be revised, and students generate ideas for making their paper more interesting to the reader. The paper is then revised and written on a final think-sheet that is simply a blank sheet of lined white paper.

Teaching the Strategy

Teaching the POWER explanation strategy involves the following four steps.

Step 1. The teacher begins instruction by examining the characteristics of good explanations. Using an overhead projector, the teacher presents students' writing that illustrates good and poor examples of explanations. The teacher leads a think-aloud discussion on the characteristics of these papers, emphasizing the structure of the text and the elements of writing that promote high-quality writing.

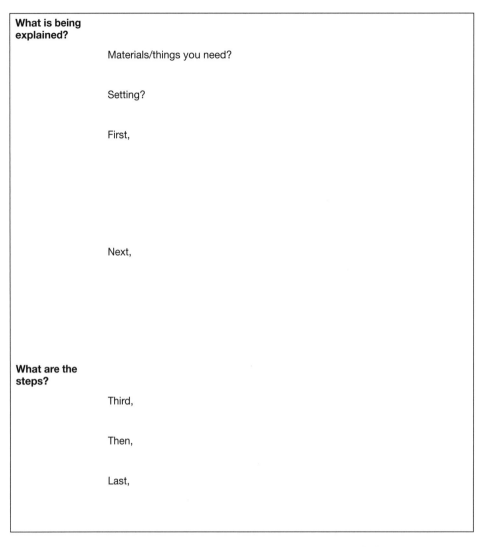

What is being explained?

Materials/things you need?

Setting?

First,

Next,

What are the steps?

Third,

Then,

Last,

Figure 12.2.   Organize think-sheet: Explanation paper. (*Source:* Englert, Raphael, Anderson, Anthony, & Stevens [1991].)

For example, the teacher may think aloud about the type of text structure used in a particular paper, elements that aid comprehension (e.g., key words such as "first" and "second"), and the types of questions the text was designed to answer. The teacher also thinks aloud about any part of the text that is difficult to understand and why. The teacher and students then try to determine what types of information the writer might have provided to solve the teacher's difficulty with the text. Next, students help the teacher apply this same kind of analyses to four explanation papers that differ in overall quality. As they work through these four papers, students increasingly take responsibility for leading the discussion.

Author's name: _____

Read to check information.

What is my paper mainly about?

What do I like best? Put a * next to the best part and explain why.

What parts are not clear? Put a ? next to the unclear parts, and tell why they are not clear.

Is the paper interesting? Tell why or why not.

Question yourself to check organization.

Did I:

Tell what was being explained?	Yes	Sort of	No
Tell what things you need?	Yes	Sort of	No
Make the steps clear?	Yes	Sort of	No
Use keywords (first, second)?	Yes	Sort of	No
Make it interesting?	Yes	Sort of	No

Plan revisions. (look back)

What parts do I want to change?

1. _____

2. _____

Write two or more questions for my editor.

1. _____

2. _____

Figure 12.3.   Editing think-sheet for the writer: Explanation paper. (*Source:* Englert & Mariage [1991].)

Step 2. The teacher models how to use each phase of POWER to write an explanation using the think-sheets presented in Figures 12.1 through 12.5. The think-sheets are described as an aid to help writers record their plans and thinking so that they can refer to them later. While modeling, the teacher demonstrates the self-talk, questions, and strategies students need to use in that phase of writing (e.g., planning an explanation). In addition, the teacher and students discuss when the strategies in that phase should be used and why they are important.

Step 3. After modeling a particular phase of the strategy (e.g., planning), students participate in a dialogue as they apply the procedures in that phase to construct a class paper. The teacher records students' ideas on the think-sheet, provides assistance, and directs the dialogue only as needed. Additional guided practice is provided as students are asked to apply the strategy to a topic of their own choosing. To facilitate dialogue, students have conferences with each other and share their thoughts and ideas as they move through each phase of the strategy. The teacher further fosters dialogue about the POWER explanation

Author's name: _____   Editor's name: _____

Read to check information. (Author: Read your paper aloud to your editor.)

What is the paper mainly about?

What do I like best? Put a * next to the part you liked best and tell why you like it here:

What parts are not clear? Put a ? next to the unclear parts, and tell what made the part not clear.

Is the paper interesting? Tell why or why not here:

Question yourself to check organization.
Did the author:

Tell what things you need?	Yes	Sort of	No
Use keywords (first, second)?	Yes	Sort of	No

Plan for editing conference.
What two parts do you think should be changed or revised? (For anything marked "Sort of" or "No," should the author add to, take out, reorder?)

1. _____

2. _____

What could help make the paper more interesting?

Talk.
Talk to the author of the paper. Talk about your comments on this editing think-sheet. Share ideas for revising the paper.

Figure 12.4.   Editing think-sheet for the peer editor: Comparison/contrast paper. (*Source:* Englert & Mariage [1991].)

strategy by displaying via an overhead projector examples of how students used the strategy. The class discussion focuses on the decisions the writer made, problems encountered, and possible alternative responses or strategies.

Step 4. After being guided to use the strategy to write a class paper and a composition on a topic of their own choosing, students are encouraged to use the procedures more independently. The teacher continues to provide needed help until the students can apply the POWER explanation strategy independently.

What to Expect

The POWER explanation strategy was validated with fourth- and fifth-grade students with learning disabilities (Englert et al., 1991). The participating school district had

Author's name: _____

List suggestions from your editor.

1. _____

2. _____

3. _____

4. _____

5. _____

Decide on the suggestions to use.
    Put a * next to all the suggestions that you will use in revising your paper.

Think about making your paper more interesting.
    List ideas for making your paper more interesting to your reader.

Return to your first draft.
    On your first draft, make all changes that you think will improve your paper. Use ideas from the lists you have made on this think-sheet.

Figure 12.5.   Revision think-sheet: Explanation paper. (*Source:* Raphael, Englert, & Murphy [1989].)

identified all students as having a learning disability. School criteria for identifying students with learning disabilities included average intelligence, a significant discrepancy between ability and achievement, and no evidence of any other disability. The only norm-referenced data provided were in the area of reading. On a group-administered reading test, students with learning disabilities scored at about the mid-second-grade level.

Learning to use the POWER explanation strategy had a positive impact on papers written by these students. In comparison to students with learning disabilities who received process writing instruction (Graves, 1983), students who received strategy instruction wrote explanations that were higher quality, contained more ideas, and were more sensitive to the needs of the reader. Unfortunately, standard deviations were not reported, making it impossible to calculate effect sizes. A concrete example of the effects of the strategy, however, is provided in the following two explanations about football written by a child with learning disabilities, the first written before instruction and the second after (from Englert et al., 1988, p. 110).

Before instruction:

How to Throw a Football

1. Pick up the football.

2. Put your fingers on the laces.

3. Put the football back of your head.

4. Then throw the football.

Tip 1: Teachers can increase students' motivation to the use the POWER explanation strategy by emphasizing its positive effects on writing. This can include asking students to select their best explanation produced when using the strategy and displaying it in a prominent place in the classroom.

Tip 2: Encourage students to check and see if their explanation works. This can include having them, the peer editor, or another student test it out. Of course, some children's explanations cannot be tested, such as this one: "Cure for a toothache: Take a mouthful of cold water and sit on the stove until it boils."

Tip 3: Students may need more than the five steps included in Figure 12.2 to organize ideas for their explanation. We recommend that alternative organization think-sheets be available for such occasions.

After instruction:

How to Play Football

I am going to explain how to play football. First you need the people. like a coach, referee, players, fans, and the quarterback. You need people to play football.

Then you need the equipment like a helmet, football, shoes, uniform with a number, kneepads, and shoulder pads.

Now you need a place. An indoor field or an outdoor field. Finally, you need the rules like face mask and holding.

To choose who gets the ball, one team chooses heads or tails. Then they flip the coin. One team kicks the ball. They try to get 6 points. It's called a touchdown. To get a first down, you get 4 tries. Where the person gets tackled is where the ball is played. The team passes or runs the ball until they get past the end zone. This is called a touchdown. They get six points for a touchdown. Then they can go for 2 points or 1 point. If you make a touchdown, you get 6 points and go for 1 point.

Portability

The POWER explanation strategy is effective not only with fourth- and fifth-grade students with learning disabilities but also with their fourth- and fifth-grade peers with typical achievement (Englert et al., 1991). After instruction in the strategy, the explanations produced by readers with and without learning disabilities improved. Their explanations were higher quality, contained more ideas, and were increasingly sensitive to the needs of the reader. With some modifications, we think that the strategy can be applied with second- and third-grade children as well. Some modifications may include making the planning, editing, and revising think-sheets less complex. For example, we would include the who, why, and what prompts on the planning think-sheet (see Figure 12.1) but eliminate the how prompt for younger students. Similarly, on the edit sheet completed by the author, we would reduce the number of questions to check organization that younger children complete (see Figure 12.3).

Extensions

One way that the POWER explanation strategy can be extended is by taking the basic organizational structure provided by POWER to plan, organize, write, edit, and revise, along with the corresponding think-sheets, and adapt them so that they are appropriate for other genres. In the next chapter, we see how Englert and her colleagues (1991) did this with comparison/contrast papers. This same basic approach can be applied to other genres such as stories, personal narratives, persuasive essays, descriptions, and so forth. For example, POWER can be adapted so that students learn to write papers that organize their observations about cause and effect. For writing an observational report about science experiments, for example, the planning think-sheet might include prompts about the question being answered, predictions, methods, and needed materials. The organizational think-sheet might include a graphic organizer that students use to record each cause and effect tested, as well as their observations about each test. Questions on the edit think-sheets might focus on student's description of the experiment (e.g., questions, predictions, methods materials, cause and effect observations, conclusions), identification of parts in need of additional work, and questions for the editing conference.

A second way of extending the POWER explanation strategy is to modify it so that it can be used to explain more complex phenomena. One way to do this is to change the organizational think-sheet. A more complex organizer (e.g., 10 steps with spaces for substeps) is substituted for the simple five-step structure presented in Figure 12.2. Teachers should carefully monitor the effectiveness of these extensions and the modifications suggested previously (see Chapter 17).

Before moving to the next chapter, we would like to share two additional child-generated explanations that provide an alternative view on how a whistle works and why a grasshopper is nervous.

> When we blow into a whistle, the air is pushed together in some places and pulled apart in others. Naturally, it screams and that is the sound we hear.

> A grasshopper is nervous and jumps because he cannot sleep. He cannot sleep because he has no eyelids. He has no eyelids because he is too nervous and jumpy to sleep.

CHAPTER 13

Writing a Comparison/ Contrast Paper

Joyce Carol Oates describes her writing as "heavy engineering," employing reams of notes as well as charts and graphs. The novelist Frank Yerby uses a similar metaphor, indicating that writing a novel is "like building a wall brick by brick; only amateurs believe in inspiration." Sam Shepard, the playwright and actor, is not content with just planning and building the wall, however. He tests his initial drafts by having it acted out, directly observing any flaws, and soliciting feedback from the actors before making needed revisions.

In contrast, students with learning disabilities do not typically employ such a methodical approach (Graham, Harris, & Troia, 1998). When writing papers that compare and contrast two events, for example, they often generate a composition off the top of their heads without the benefit of first systematically analyzing how the events are similar and different or how their thoughts can be organized. Students with learning disabilities are also unlikely to test the veracity of their claims once these ideas are recorded on paper. This extemporaneous approach to composing can yield some unusual comparisons.

> Dogs are much quicker than people. In less than 2 months, they are a year older.

> The different kind of senses are commonsense and nonsense.

> During the cold winter months, the days get cold and contract. In the summer time they get hot and expand.

The *POWER comparison/contrast strategy* provides one antidote to these types of errors. It is a systematic procedure for planning and building the comparison/contrast wall and testing its veracity.

THE POWER STRATEGY FOR
WRITING COMPARISONS/CONTRASTS

The POWER comparison/contrast strategy provides a structure that prompts students to *plan* and *organize* their comparison papers in advance of writing, use this plan and organizational structure to *write* a first draft, *evaluate* the substance of their first draft (with help from a peer), and execute *revisions* designed to make the comparisons better and more interesting (Englert, Raphael, & Anderson, 1992; Englert, Raphael, Anderson, Anthony, & Stevens, 1991; Raphael, Englert, & Kirschner, 1989). The strategy further supports each of these writing phases by teaching students strategic moves for carrying out these processes. The steps for writing a compare/contrast paper with POWER are presented in the following steps. (The strategy is similar to the POWER explanation strategy presented in Chapter 12.)

Step 1. Plan: The first step is to develop a plan for writing the compare/contrast paper. This includes identifying what is to be compared and contrasted ("Joe and I"), who will read it ("Joe"), establishing a purpose for writing it ("so Joe and I will know how we are the same and different"), brainstorming ideas about the topic, and grouping these ideas into relevant categories. The think-sheet for this step is presented in Figure 13.1.

Step 2. Organize: The second step, organize, involves developing a text structure map that categorizes and orders students' ideas (see Figure 13.2). Students re-identify what is being compared and contrasted ("Joe and I") and on what dimen-

---

Author's name: _____   Date: _____

Topic: _____

Who: Who am I writing for?   _____

Why: Why am I writing this?   _____

What: What do I already know about my topic? (Brainstorm)

1. _____

2. _____

3. _____

4. _____

How: How do I group my ideas?

Writing Better: Effective Strategies for Teaching Students with Learning Difficulties, by S. Graham and K.R. Harris,
© 2005 Paul H. Brookes Publishing Co., Inc. All rights reserved.

Figure 13.1.   Planning think-sheet: Comparison/contrast paper. (From Raphael, Englert, & Murphy [1989].)

What is being compared/contrasted?		
On what?		
	Alike?	Different?
On what?		
	Alike?	Different?
On what?		
	Alike?	Different?

Figure 13.2.   Organizing think-sheet: Comparison/contrast paper (From Raphael, Englert, & Murphy [1989].)

sions ("size and looks"). Next, students organize how the two items are alike and different on each of these selected dimensions.

Step 3. Write: With the third step, write, students use the text structure map as a guide for writing a first draft. Students flesh out the map by adding an introduction, conclusion, details, key words, examples, and so forth. The think-sheet for this step is a blank sheet of lined colored paper, instead of white paper, to remind students that this is not the final draft.

Step 4. Edit: The fourth step, edit, involves peer editing. Using the think-sheet in Figure 13.3 as a guide, the writer reflects on the first draft, identifying favorite parts, parts that need work, and questions to discuss with the peer editor. Conjointly, the peer editor uses the think-sheet in Figure 12.4 to identify strengths and weaknesses. Both students place stars next to the parts they liked best and question marks by the parts that are confusing. They then meet to discuss the paper and how to improve it.

Step 5. Revise: With the aid of a revision think-sheet (see Figure 13.5), students consider how best to revise the paper. They list the editing suggestions generated and received during Step 4 and decide which revisions to implement. A star is placed next to each suggestion that will be revised, and students generate ideas

Author's name: _____

Read to check information.

   What is my paper mainly about?

   What do I like best? Put a * next to the best part and explain why.

   What parts are not clear? Put a ? next to the unclear parts, and tell why they are not clear.

   Is the paper interesting? Tell why or why not.

Question yourself to check organization.
Did I:

Tell what was being explained?	Yes	Sort of	No
Tell what things you need?	Yes	Sort of	No
Make the steps clear?	Yes	Sort of	No
Use keywords (first, second)?	Yes	Sort of	No
Make it interesting?	Yes	Sort of	No

Plan revisions. (look back)
What parts do I want to change?

1. _____

2. _____

Write two or more questions for my editor.

1. _____

2. _____

Figure 13.3.   Editing think-sheet for the writer: Comparison/contrast paper. (From Raphael, Englert, & Murphy [1989].)

for making their paper more interesting to the reader. The paper is then revised and written on a final think-sheet that is simply a blank sheet of lined white paper.

Teaching the Strategy

Teaching the POWER comparison/contrast strategy involves four steps. These are the same steps used to teach the POWER Explanation (see Chapter 12). These steps are again described here, focusing on their application to writing a comparison paper.

Step 1. The teacher begins instruction by examining the characteristics of a good comparison/contrast paper. Using an overhead projector, the teacher presents students' writing that illustrate good and poor examples of such papers. The teacher leads a think-aloud discussion on the characteristics of these papers, emphasizing the structure of the text and the elements of writing that promote quality. For example, the teacher might think aloud about the types of key words used in such a composition (e.g., *same* and *different*) or the kinds of questions this sort of text is designed to answer. The teacher also points out any part of

Author's name: _____   Editor's name: _____

Read to check information. (Authors: Read your paper aloud to your editor.)

What is the paper mainly about?

What do I like best? Put a * next to the part you liked best and tell why you like it here:

What parts are not clear? Put a ? next to the unclear parts, and tell what made the part not clear.

Is the paper interesting? Tell why or why not here:

Question yourself to check organization.
Did the author:

Tell what two things are compared and contrasted?	Yes	Sort of	No
Tell things they are being compared and contrasted on?	Yes	Sort of	No
Tell how they are alike?	Yes	Sort of	No
Tell how they are different?	Yes	Sort of	No
Use keywords clearly?	Yes	Sort of	No

Plan for editing conference.
What two parts do you think should be changed or revised? (For anything marked "Sort of" or "No," should the author add to, take out, reorder?)

1. _____

2. _____

What could help make the paper more interesting?

Talk.

Talk to the author of the paper. Talk about your comments on this editing think-sheet. Share ideas for revising the paper.

Figure 13.4. Editing think-sheet for the peer editor: Comparison/contrast paper. (From Raphael, Englert, & Murphy [1989].)

the text that is difficult to understand and why. Teacher and students then try to determine what types of information the writer might have provided to make this segment of text more understandable. Next, students help the teacher apply this same kind of analysis to four additional comparison/contrast papers that differ in overall quality. As they work through these four papers, students increasingly take responsibility for leading the discussion.

Step 2. The teacher models how to use each phase of POWER to write a comparison/contrast paper using the think-sheets presented in Figures 13.1 through 13.4. The think-sheets are an aid to help writers record their plans and thoughts as

Tip 1: When asked to name six animals peculiar to the Arctic, a student wrote, "three bears and three seals." Like this child, some students have difficulty generating ideas for their compositions. One way to tackle this problem is to have them work with a peer or in a small group as they complete the plan and organize think-sheets.

Tip 2: Students may need more than the three "On what" comparisons included in Figure 13.2 to organize ideas for their explanation. We recommend that alternative organization think-sheets be available for such occasions.

Tip 3: Once students can easily and correctly use the POWER comparison/contrast strategy, teachers should encourage them to apply the strategy without using the think-sheets. Instead, students should be encouraged to write their thoughts and ideas for each phase of the strategy on regular paper. This will make the strategy more portable.

they work on each phase of composing. While modeling, the teacher demonstrates the self-talk, questions, and strategies students need to use in that phase of writing (e.g., organizing information for a comparison/contrast paper). In addition, the teacher and students discuss when the strategies in that phase should be used and why they are important.

Step 3. After modeling a particular phase of the strategy (e.g., organizing), students apply the procedures in that stage to construct a class paper. The teacher records

Author's name: _____

List suggestions from your editor.

1. _____

2. _____

3. _____

4. _____

5. _____

Decide on the suggestions to use.

　　Put a * next to all the suggestions that you will use in revising your paper.

Think about making your paper more interesting.

　　List ideas for making your paper more interesting to your reader.

Return to your first draft.

　　On your first draft, make all changes that you think will improve your paper. Use ideas from the lists you have made on this think-sheet.

Writing Better: Effective Strategies for Teaching Students with Learning Difficulties, by S. Graham and K.R. Harris, © 2005 Paul H. Brookes Publishing Co., Inc. All rights reserved.

Figure 13.5. Revision think-sheet: Comparison/contrast paper. (From Raphael, Englert, & Murphy [1989].)

students' ideas on the think-sheet, providing assistance, and directing their discussion only as needed. Additional guided practice is provided as students are asked to apply the strategy to a topic of their own choosing. To facilitate discussion about what they are doing, students have conferences with each other and share their thoughts and ideas as they move through each phase of the strategy. The teacher fosters further dialogue about the POWER comparison/contrast strategy by displaying on an overhead projector examples of how students used the strategy. The class discussion focuses on the decisions the writer made, problems encountered, and possible alternative responses or strategies.

Step 4. After being guided to use the strategy to write a class paper and a composition of their own choosing, students are encouraged to use the procedures more independently. The teacher continues to provide needed help until the student can apply the POWER comparison/contrast strategy independently.

What to Expect

The POWER comparison/contrast strategy was validated with fourth- and fifth-grade students identified by their school district as having a learning disability (Englert et al., 1991). School criteria for identifying students as having a learning disability included average intelligence, a significant discrepancy between ability and achievement, and no evidence of any other disability. The only norm-referenced data provided were in the area of reading. On a group-administered reading test, students with learning disabilities scored at about the mid–second-grade level.

Learning to use the POWER comparison/contrast strategy had a positive impact on these students' papers (Englert et al., 1991). In comparison with students with learning disabilities who received process writing instruction (Graves, 1983), students who received strategy instruction wrote comparison/contrast papers that were higher quality, contained more ideas, and were more sensitive to the needs of the reader. Unfortunately, standard deviations were not reported, making it impossible to calculate effect sizes.

Portability

In addition to being effective with fourth- and fifth-grade students with learning disabilities, the POWER comparison/contrast strategy works well with other children in these grades. Englert and her colleagues (1991) found that the strategy improved the writing of both weaker and stronger readers in fourth- and fifth-grade classrooms of children without learning disabilities. After instruction, their comparison/contrast papers were rated as being higher quality, richer in ideas, and more sensitive to readers' needs.

Extensions

One way that the POWER comparison/contrast strategy can be extended is by providing more specific guidance on how to make comparisons. For example, the organize think-sheet could encourage students to make comparisons based on size, weight, sight, sound, taste, touch, purpose, and so forth. In some cases, the attributes to be compared and contrasted may need to be even more specific. For example, if the writing assignment directs students to examine the similarities and differences between mammals and birds, the organize think-sheet might encourage students to focus on even more specific characteristics such as being warm blooded versus being cold blooded and laying eggs versus giving live birth. In other cases, a more open-ended graphic organizer, such as a Venn diagram, might be preferable. In any event, teachers need to monitor the effectiveness of such modifications (see Chapter 17).

Before ending this chapter, we would like to share some more child-generated comparisons.

> The difference between bones and skeletons are the same except we live ones have bones while dead ones have skeletons.

> Axioms and postulates are the same. We have them both in case we forget the word for one of them.

> New York is better than Los Angeles because you can get out of school there sometimes. Los Angeles don't have blizzards or snow or anything swell like that.

CHAPTER 14

Report Writing

The journalist Stanley Karnow, author of *Vietnam: A History*, indicated that before gathering information on his topic he first developed a roadmap, integrating what he knew and where he wanted to go. This initial outline changed and grew as he more fully researched the topic.

When students with learning disabilities are asked to develop a report on a topic, they often do little actual research, relying more on their incomplete and sometimes inaccurate knowledge to write their paper (Graham, 1990; Thomas, Englert, & Gregg, 1987). This is illustrated in this rather humorous, but confused, report on dairy cows.

> There's this big brown cow with the red eyes and wet tongue and he has a balloon under him full of nibbles, The man gets a pail of milk and a fire hose, and they put the fire hose on one of the nibbles and the other end in the pail of milk. They then turn the machine on and fill the cow full of milk.

The *report writing strategy* presented in this chapter is similar to the approach employed by Stanley Karnow. Students first develop a map of what they already know and still need to learn about a topic. They then gather additional information about the topic, modifying and upgrading the map so that it more fully and accurately fits their evolving grasp of the subject. The resulting map serves as an outline or guide for writing the paper.

REPORT WRITING STRATEGY

Students with learning disabilities often have to write reports for social studies, science, or English. This may involve writing a paper on a contemporary figure such as

Martin Luther King, Jr., a country such as Egypt, or a process such as habitat loss. Report writing typically requires that students generate and organize information from multiple sources. This includes information obtained from written sources and interviews, as well as what they already know. The student must sift, analyze, cull, and organize this information in order to write an effective report.

The report writing strategy helps students carry out each of these processes and more (MacArthur, Schwartz, Graham, Molloy, & Harris, 1996). Students gather information through brainstorming, reading, and interviewing. Collected information is displayed on a map that shows the relationships between important concepts and details. The map is updated and modified as new information is gathered and students' understanding of the topic changes. The map is used as a resource and guide and may be revised further once the student starts writing. The strategy involves the following six steps.

Step 1. Students first brainstorm what they already know about the topic of their report and identify other areas or concepts where information is needed. For example, a student working on a report on lemurs started by listing that they are monkeys with large eyes and ringed tails, are active at night, live in trees, and are found in jungles and zoos. Although the student's knowledge about lemurs was limited and not completely accurate, it provided a starting point for thinking about what else he needed to know. With this in mind, he listed five things he wanted to learn more about: what they look like, where they live, what they eat, if they can be pets, and what their habits are.

Step 2. Students then take their lists of what they know and what they want to learn and organize this information on a map or chart. This can be done as a web (see Figure 14.1) or any other type of graphic display that shows the relationship between ideas. Students are encouraged to place items on their map as either a main idea or a detail. In Figure 14.1, main ideas are circled and details are listed on lines next to them.

Step 3. Students next gather additional information about their topic. Pertinent information is added to the map, inaccuracies are deleted or corrected (e.g., lemurs are only *related* to monkeys), categories are revised or rearranged, and so forth. Information can be taken from a variety of sources including books, encyclopedias, magazines, and interviews. As students gather new information, they ask themselves three questions:

- What do I want to know?
- What is the main point of this section (or speaker)?
- Is this information on my map?

Step 4. Once students are ready to write, the map provides a resource that summarizes what they know about the topic. Before writing, they organize this information by numbering which main idea will come first, second, third, and so forth.

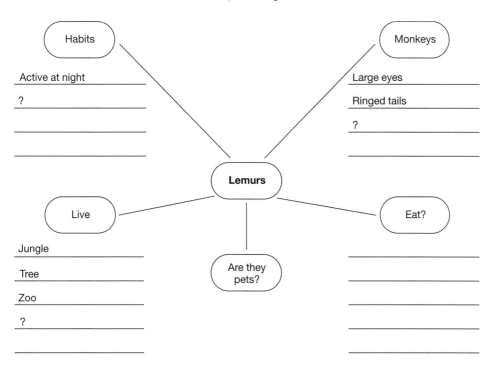

Figure 14.1. Map of "What I know and what I want to learn about lemurs."

Step 5. Students are encouraged to continue the process of planning as they write. This includes stopping to locate additional information, confirming the accuracy of a particular piece of information, reorganizing their paper's format, and so forth.

Step 6. Students are further encouraged to consult their map to ensure that they included all of the information they planned to use. A checkmark is placed next to each item as it is included in the report.

Teaching the Strategy

General procedures for teaching the report writing strategy are described in Chapter 3. Consequently, only instructional procedures specific to this strategy are presented here.

Report writing is a complex strategy requiring the use and coordination of a variety of processes and skills, including brainstorming, webbing, reading to locate information, interviewing, and conceptualizing and categorizing information as main ideas and details. For students with learning disabilities, at least at the fourth-grade level, it may take as much as 3–4 months for them to learn to use this strategy effectively (MacArthur et al., 1996). This is partly because it takes students 1–2 weeks to write a report, and they need to apply the strategy multiple times to master it. We think this investment of time is well worth it, however, because report writing is a skill that students will use throughout their academic career.

It is easier to teach the report writing strategy if students are already familiar with brainstorming, webbing, gathering information from reading material, categorizing

Tip 1: Students may decide to combine strategy Steps 1 and 2 by mapping or webbing what they know and want to know while brainstorming these ideas. This does not present a problem as long as the process of mapping ideas does not interfere with the process of generating them.

Tip 2: One of the most challenging aspects of the report writing strategy is transforming and organizing gathered information into main ideas and details (Step 3), as illustrated by the following student mistake: "Veterinarians are animals that were in the war. "Some students may require additional guided practice to master these skills.

Tip 3: Another way to reduce the complexity of the strategy is to initially limit sources for gathering information to either reading materials or interviews.

ideas, and interviewing. We recommend these processes be taught before students learn to use the strategy.

The teacher introduces the report writing strategy with a discussion of what students know about reports and what makes a good report. Using a chart (see Figure 14.2), the teacher describes how each step of the strategy operates and emphasizes how the steps are interrelated.

Before modeling how to use the strategy, some teachers find it helpful to provide additional discussion on the attributes of a good report. One way to do this is by asking students to read a model report and then discuss the organizational and informational qualities that make it a good paper. These attributes should be listed on a chart that is displayed prominently in the classroom.

While modeling how to use the strategy, the teacher involves students whenever possible. This includes brainstorming as a class what students know and want to learn about the topic, helping the teacher organize this information on the web, gathering their own

1. Brainstorm what you know and what you want to learn.

2. Organize your information on a map or web.

3. Gather new information and revise your map or web.

4. Number what will go first, second, third, and so forth.

5. Use the map or web as you write and keep planning.

6. Check the map or web: Did you write what you wanted to?

Figure 14.2.   Chart for the report writing strategy.

information to include on the web, assisting in sequencing information for writing, help-ing the teacher draft the report, and checking to see that all pertinent information is included.

As students start to practice using the strategy more independently, we typically ask two or three students to work together to prepare a report. After two or three reports, most students are ready to apply the strategy individually.

What to Expect

The report writing strategy was validated with a class of fourth-grade students who were team-taught by a special education teacher and a reading specialist (MacArthur et al., 1996). All but one of the students had been identified as having a learning disability. The other student was classified as having a language disability. Students' scores on an indi-vidually administered intelligence test ranged from 97 to 126. Students' performance on an individually administered writing measure was 1–2 *standard deviations* below the test mean. Four of the students in this class also took medication for attention-deficit/hyper-activity disorder, and one of the students had cerebral palsy.

In contrast to the other writing strategies described in this book, the effects of the report writing strategy were examined using qualitative research methods. Students were, however, asked to write a report before and after instruction. Analysis of the stu-dents' papers showed that there was an improvement in the quality, organization, and content of their reports after instruction. The two papers below provide a concrete illus-tration of these changes. Both of these papers were corrected for spelling, punctuation, and capitalization miscues.

Before instruction:

What I know about forest fires is that they began by lightning or by somebody throwing match and forget to put it out. Sometimes because they throw cigarettes or they forget to put the camping fire out. And I thought that forest fires were all bad for forest. What I didn't know was that some forest fires were good for the forest and that Yellow Stone park was a place where lots of forest fires occurred.

After instruction:

Germs

Germs are tiny cells that get into people's body and make you look sick. Who get germs? People like us get germs on your hands, from cats and dogs, and lots of other places like which fight germs. White blood that your blood has works very hard to kill germs.

How do you feel? You feel like throwing up; you feel sick; stomach aches come to you; you get fever, pain, breaks, aches, and rashes. You feel all these things when you have germs inside your body.

From where do they come? They come from old metal and dirt. There is even germs in food, in the air, from the hands. There is even germs in water, and everything that you touch that is not clean.

What happens when you have germs? You cough, you get allergies, you get a cold, you have a feeling to throw-up. That all happens when you have germs in your body. All things that you read here comes from germs in your body. The skin is your protection against germs.

Portability

The report writing strategy has only been tested with a single class of fourth-grade students with learning disabilities. Even so, we expect that this strategy would be effective with most other students in fourth through sixth grades. The process of writing a report is a complicated and demanding task that is quite challenging for most students. The report writing strategy provides a logical and reasonable framework for accomplishing this task. One caution is in order, however. For it to be effective, teachers must provide students with enough time and practice to fully master the strategy.

Extensions

We offer three suggestions for making the report writing strategy more responsive to the demands of assignments in different content area. First, writing a good report involves judging the value and veracity of one's own ideas as well as the ideas of others. Teachers can help students acquire these skills through modeling and discussion. Second, sources of information differ from one discipline to another. Students often require teacher guidance in how to access relevant resources when gathering information in different content areas. Third, students need to learn different methods for charting information. For example, if a student is writing a report comparing how ancient Egyptians cared for the Nile River with how modern Americans take care of the Mississippi River, a graphic organizer that helps the writer clarify differences and similarities may be preferable to a semantic web.

Finally, just in case you didn't learn enough about cows at the beginning of this chapter, we close by sharing some other child-generated "cow facts."

The cow gives us milk. A young cow is called a calf and gives us jelly.

To keep milk from going sour, you should keep it in the cow.

The cow has six sides: right, left, fore, back, upper, and below.

The cow has a fine sense of smell and you can smell it far away. That is the reason for fresh air in the country.

SECTION V

Strategies for Self-Regulating
and the Writing Process

Several years ago, we observed a young child as he tried to put a puzzle together. One of the pieces of the puzzle didn't fit right, and he got more and more frustrated trying to finish it. Each time his anger rose to the point where he was about to sweep all of the pieces off of the table, he pushed his chair back and said, "I'm not going to get mad because mad makes me do bad." Although he never did get all of the pieces to fit, he maintained his cool and kept at it for quite a long time.

The self-instruction that this child used to regulate his emotions is an example of a self-regulation strategy. *Self-regulation* refers to the thoughts, feelings, and actions that people use to obtain some desired goal (Schunk & Zimmerman, 1994). Strategies for self-regulation also include self-reinforcement, self-monitoring, and goal setting. We integrated these self-regulation procedures into the SRSD model presented in Chapter 3 to help students manage the writing process, their writing behavior, and the planning, writing, or revising strategies that they learn. Self-regulation strategies such as self-monitoring and goal setting, however, do not have to be part of a larger instructional package to be effective (Graham & Harris, 1997c). Many writers have used goal setting, for example, to help them be productive (Zimmerman & Reisemberg, 1997). After getting married, Philip K. Dick, the author of *Do Androids Dream of Electric Sheep?*, set a goal to write two novels per year. He made this goal a reality by writing every morning, often producing the first draft of a novel in 6 weeks and editing it in another 6 weeks. Emile Zola was no less successful, with his goal, "No day without lines"; he produced 1,500 words per day, resulting in almost 50 books.

In this section, we examine how self-monitoring (Chapter 15) and goal setting (Chapter 16) can help students with learning disabilities write better. Each self-monitoring or goal-setting strategy is first described. Procedures for teaching it, as well as scientific evidence on its effectiveness, are then examined. (As a reminder, an effect size of .20 is considered small, .50 is medium, and .80 is large.) Finally, we identify other students who might profit from learning the strategy and how its use can be extended and modified.

CHAPTER 15

Self-Monitoring

One of America's greatest writers, Ernest Hemingway, placed great store in the power of monitoring how much he wrote. Every day he recorded his progress on a large piece of cardboard so that he could eliminate any self-deception about his productivity. Anthony Trollope, author of more than 50 novels, used an even more elaborate system to establish discipline over his writing. With stopwatch in hand, he counted the number of words written every 15 minutes. This helped him write regularly, day in and day out.

Counting and recording writing output helped these two novelists stay focused and remain productive. This same strategy can also help struggling writers by increasing how much they write as well as their on-task behavior while composing (Harris, Graham, Reid, McElroy, & Hamby, 1994). In this chapter, we describe how this strategy can be applied with students with learning disabilities. We then examine a second validated strategy that focuses on counting and recording the basic structural elements in a composition. Although this strategy can be applied to a variety of genres, it has only been validated empirically with story writing. As a result, we describe how to use it when writing this type of paper but provide suggestions for extending its use to at least one other genre.

STRATEGY 1: SELF-MONITORING AND RECORDING WRITING OUTPUT

Self-monitoring and recording writing output involves three steps.

Step 1. After writing, students count the number of words in their composition. All words are counted, including title and ending. Words are counted even if they are spelled incorrectly.

Step 2. Students record the number of words they wrote on a personal bar or graph chart that they keep in their writing folder.

Step 3. Each time they write a new composition, students compare their current performance to their output on previous compositions. This provides them with an indication of whether their writing output is increasing, decreasing, or remaining steady over time.

Figure 15.1 provides an example of a recording chart that we use with students with learning disabilities. The chart contains five rockets, and each rocket represents a single composition. To the side of each rocket is a number scale, starting at 0 at the rocket's base and increasing to over 100 at its tip. This scale can be adjusted to fit each students' typical output. To illustrate, the scale might range from 0 to 60 for a child who commonly generates about 30 words per paper. Whenever a student completes a composition, he or she counts the number of words produced and uses a marker or crayon to color the rocket up to that numerical point.

Teaching the Strategy

Students with learning disabilities can be taught how to use self-monitoring and recording of writing output in 15–20 minutes. We use the following steps to teach this procedure (Harris et al., 1994).

Step 1. The teacher and students first discuss the importance of writing longer papers. When writing a story, for example, additional content makes the story more complete and better.

Step 2. Next, the teacher tells the students that they will learn a strategy (or trick) that will help them write longer papers. The teacher describes the strategy using a chart that briefly describes each step (see Figure 15.2). The teacher explains that

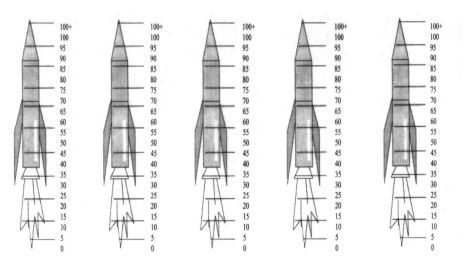

Figure 15.1.   Rocket graphs for recording number of words.

Tip 1: Teachers may need to help some younger children count the number of words written and chart the score.

Tip 2: Teachers may be able to increase the effectiveness of this strategy by asking students to set a goal to write even more words in their next composition. The goal should be concrete, specifying how many words will be written (e.g., 142 words). It should also be challenging, resulting in at least a 10% increase in writing output. Students should record the goal on their charts and check to see if it is met when they do their next composition.

Tip 3: Longer compositions are not always better compositions. For some students, it may be necessary to provide feedback about the quality of their compositions as they start to write longer papers. This should include identifying with the student any content that either enhances or disrupts the quality of the composition.

---

keeping track of how many words they write will encourage them to include more ideas in their writing.

Step 3. Using the chart as a guide, the teacher shows students how to use the strategy. This can be done using either a student paper or one that the teacher wrote.

Step 4. Students then practice using the strategy with a paper they wrote previously. They are encouraged to follow the steps on the chart. (Individual charts can be made for students, if necessary.) As students practice using the strategy, the teacher provides any needed assistance. This continues until students can use the strategy independently.

Step 5. After this initial session, the teacher monitors students' use of the strategy, providing help as needed. The teacher holds frequent conferences with each child to check and see whether the strategy is having the desired effect and to make any necessary adjustments.

When writing stories, the on-task behavior of the students who were taught to use the self-monitoring strategy jumped from 50% to 80%. There was also a corresponding gain in how much these students wrote because story length increased by 160%. Even more important, the overall quality of stories improved as a result of counting and recording the number of words written. Students indicated that they liked using the strategy and that it helped them with their writing. For example, one student indicated that if he stopped using self-monitoring, the quality of his stories would deteriorate; another child noted that he would not write as much.

---

1. After writing, I count how many words I wrote.

2. I graph how many words I wrote.

3. I ask, "Is it more words or fewer words than I wrote last time?"

Writing Better: Effective Strategies for Teaching Students with Learning Difficulties, by S. Graham and K.R. Harris,
© 2005 Paul H. Brookes Publishing Co., Inc. All rights reserved.
Figure 15.2. Chart for counting and recording number of words.

What to Expect

This strategy was validated with fifth- and sixth-grade students with learning disabilities receiving special education services in a resource room setting (Harris et al., 1994). They learned to use the strategy while writing stories. These children's scores on an individually administered intelligence test were in the average range (i.e., 85 to 115). Teachers indicated that each child had difficulty with writing, staying on task, and completing writing assignments in the classroom. The teachers' observation that each child had difficulties with writing were confirmed by scores on a standardized, norm-referenced measure of writing.

Portability

Self-monitoring and recording of writing output has been used successfully to increase the writing output of children without learning disabilities in grades 1 through 3, gifted children in grade 4, and students with behavioral difficulties in grades 4 through 6 (Moxley, Lutz, Ahlborn, Boley, & Armstrong, 1995; Rumsey & Ballard, 1985). Thus, the strategy is portable and suitable for use with students with and without special needs.

Extensions

Teachers in a study by Moxley and colleagues (1995) added an interesting embellishment to the basic strategy when they used it with their students. This included recording the total number of words written by all students on a chart, throwing a pizza party or giving extra recess time when the class total for a day reached a predetermined number (e.g., 400 words for a first-grade class with 24 students), and providing stickers or other reinforcers for individual students on each day the total reached a predetermined number (e.g., 50 words for second-grade students).

STRATEGY 2: SELF-MONITORING AND RECORDING OF STORY PARTS

In addition to monitoring and recording how much they write, students with learning disabilities can be taught to count and graph their inclusion of the basic parts or elements of a story. This strategy increases the likelihood that they will include each element in their writing, making their stories more complete. It may also stimulate them to think more fully about each part of their story.

Self-monitoring and recording of story parts involves the following two steps.

Step 1. Before writing, students take out their story checklist (see Figure 15.3). The checklist contains the following story elements: where and when the story takes place (setting), character(s), the problem (i.e., the problem that the characters are trying to solve), the plan (i.e., the goals and actions the characters put into place to solve the problem), and the ending (i.e., the result of the characters' actions).

Directions: Place a checkmark next to each story part as you include it in your story.

_____ Where and when (setting)

_____ Character(s)

_____ Problem

_____ Plan

_____ Ending

Figure 15.3. Checklist for self-monitoring and recording story parts. (Adapted from Montague & Leavell [1994].)

Step 2. While writing, students place a checkmark next to each element on the checklist as it is included in their story.

Teaching the Strategy

Students with learning disabilities can be taught how to use self-monitoring and recording of story parts in one or two sessions. The strategy is taught using the following steps.

Step 1. The teacher and students first discuss the importance of writing stories that include the most important elements. Students are told that this will make their stories more complete, elaborate, and interesting.

Step 2. Next, the teacher tells students that they will learn a strategy (or trick) that will help them write stories that contain these parts. The teacher describes the strategy, using a chart that briefly presents each step (see Figure 15.4). The teacher explains that the strategy will remind them to use each part and write more complete stories.

Step 3. Using the chart as a guide, the teacher models how to use the strategy. As she writes a story, she checks off each part on the checklist (see Figure 15.5) as it is included in the story.

Step 4. During that session or the next session, students practice using the strategy as they write a story. They are encouraged to follow the steps on the chart. (Individual charts can be made for students, if necessary.) As students practice using the strategy, the teacher provides any needed assistance. This continues until students can use the strategy independently.

Step 5. The teacher monitors students' subsequent use of the strategy, providing help as needed. The teacher holds frequent conferences with each child to see whether the strategy is having the desired effect and to make any necessary adjustments.

1. Before writing, I look at my story checklist.

2. While writing, I check each part as I use it in my story.

Figure 15.4. Chart for counting and recording story parts.

Tip 1: If students do not understand the idea captured by a specific element or are not familiar with the terminology used by the teacher, there is little value in asking them to assess and record its inclusion. Before teaching the strategy, teachers need to make sure that each student can identify these elements in fairy tales or other pertinent reading material. In our own work (Danoff, Harris, & Graham, 1993), we first defined each element and illustrated its meaning by examining narrative material that the student was currently reading. Students next worked in pairs or small groups to locate story elements in other reading material, receiving help from the teachers as needed. Using a picture as a story starter, they then generated ideas for each part. Once they could do this independently, they were ready to start self-monitoring and recording their inclusion of story parts.

Tip 2: Teachers may be able to increase the effectiveness of this strategy by also asking students to monitor and check that they made notes for each element as they initially planned their story. Students with learning disabilities can be taught to make notes for story parts as early as second grade (Harris et al., 2004). Figure 15.5 contains an example of a monitoring checklist for both planning and writing (Graves & Hauge, 1993).

Tip 3: Teachers may be able to increase students' motivation to use the strategy by having students display their overall performance on a bar char or graph.

What to Expect

This strategy was validated with fifth- and sixth-grade students with learning disabilities (Graves, Monatgue, & Wong, 1990). Prior to the start of the study, all of the students were able to generate 50 or more words when writing a story in response to a picture. Stories written before instruction also contained at least two story elements as defined by students' performance on a standardized, norm-referenced measure of writing.

When students monitored and recorded story parts, they created stories that were more complete and higher quality than those written by similar students who were not

Directions: Place a checkmark next to each story part as you include it in your story.			
	Check as I plan		Check as I write
_____	Where and when (setting)	_____	Where and when (setting)
_____	Character(s)	_____	Character(s)
_____	Problem	_____	Problem
_____	Plan	_____	Plan
_____	Ending	_____	Ending

Figure 15.5. Story checklist for planning and writing. (Modified from Graves & Hauge [1993].)

taught to use this strategy. The strategy had a strong effect on overall text quality (effect size = 2.23) and a moderate effect on the inclusion of story elements (effect size = .57).

Portability

Children with and without learning disabilities from second to fifth grade have been taught to successfully monitor and record the inclusion of basic story parts in their writing (Danoff, Harris, & Graham, 1993; Graham, Harris, & Mason, in press; Harris, Graham, & Mason, 2004; Saddler et al., 2004; Sawyer, Graham, & Harris, 1992). It is important to note, however, that these subsequent applications of this self-monitoring strategy did not examine the unique effects of self-monitoring and recording story parts on children's writing. In all cases, the strategy was used in conjunction with other techniques (see Chapter 10). When using this strategy with children other than fifth- and sixth-grade students with learning disabilities (students in the validating research study), we recommend that teachers follow the assessment guidelines contained in Chapter 17.

Extensions

We have also applied self-monitoring and recording of basic structural elements to the genre of persuasive writing. A persuasive essay typically includes the following elements (Graham, 1990):

Topic sentence. A sentence telling what the writer believes: "I believe that boys and girls should play sports together."

Reasons. Reasons that support the writer's belief: "Because they will learn to get along better"

Refutations. Refuting reasons that run counter to the writer's belief: "Girls can play sports just as well as boys."

Examples. Elaborations, examples, or conditional statements: "Except when boys cheat"

Ending. Wrapping up the argument: "These are the reasons why I think boys and girls should play sports together."

Students with learning disabilities in second through sixth grades, as well as struggling writers without a learning disability in second and third grades, have been taught to successfully monitor and record the inclusion of basic elements in their persuasive writing (De La Paz & Graham, 1997a, 1997b; Graham & Harris, 1989c; Graham et al., in press; Graham, MacArthur, Schwartz, & Page-Voth, 1992; Harris et al., 2004). The unique impact of monitoring and recording the inclusion of persuasive essay elements is unknown, however, because this procedure has always been used in conjunction with other strategies (see Chapter 11). We recommend that teachers follow the assessment guidelines contained in Chapter 17 whenever they apply this extension.

Extending Self-Monitoring More Broadly   Self-monitoring and recording can be applied to a wide range of writing skills. For example, students can count and graph the number of sentences, paragraphs, or pages produced; their use of action, describing, or transition words; and the types of revisions made (i.e., additions, deletions, substitutions, and reordering). Important aspects of the writing process can also be monitored and recorded, including issues related to structuring the writing environment, understanding the task, maintaining motivation, seeking assistance, and activating strategies for planning and revising. An illustrative list of such processes is provided in Figure 15.6.

Not all writing skills or behaviors are suitable candidates for self-monitoring and recording, as demonstrated by this student's declaration: "I have to be aware of my mistakes so that I can perfect them." We recommend that students only monitor and record instances of positive behavior, ones that are likely to improve their writing. Moreover, little is gained by teaching a student how to count and graph a behavior, such as adding text when revising, if additions are already common.

Steps for teaching students how to self-monitor and record behaviors (other than words or structural elements) are presented below. These procedures are meant to be used in a flexible manner and can be modified as needed.

Step 1. Determine and define exactly what students will self-monitor and record. This should be a behavior or event that can be defined simply and understood easily by the student. For example, "to write a good story" is a laudable goal, but it is difficult to define and measure. Remember that students must be able to assess and record the behavior or event chosen for self-monitoring.

Step 2. Gather information on the students' current performance on the behavior or event to be self-assessed. This provides evidence to support, or in some cases dismiss, the need for self-monitoring. These baseline data may also be used later to help demonstrate the benefits of self-monitoring and recording by comparing them with students' performance once they start using the strategy.

Step 3. Briefly explain the rationale for self-monitoring and recording. Describe the purpose of the strategy and the benefits students will gain from using it. Enlist students' willing cooperation and commitment to self-monitoring because it is rarely effective if students are forced to do it against their will.

Step 4. Teach the selected self-monitoring and recording procedures. It is important that students have a clear understanding of what is expected because they must learn to use the procedure independently. Thus, in this step, the teacher and students discuss *what* will be self-assessed (e.g., parts of an opinion essay), what *criteria* are desirable (to have all the basic parts), *how* to count and record the targeted aspect of writing, and *when* self-monitoring and recording are to occur (while writing). Next, the teacher (or another student proficient at self-monitoring) models how to use the procedure, verbalizing what is being done at each step. Then the teacher asks students to reiterate each step and model how to use the strategy. These last steps are important to ensure that students

Writing Process Checklist

Directions: Place a checkmark by each action that you did while writing this paper.

Time and Place

_____ I made a schedule for when I would work on the paper.

_____ I found a quiet place to write.

_____ I got started working right away.

_____ I kept track of how much time I spent working on the paper.

_____ I always had the materials I needed each time I sat down to work.

Understanding the Task

_____ I read or listened to the teacher's directions carefully.

_____ I asked the teacher to explain any part of the assignment that I did not understand.

_____ I restated the directions in my own words.

Planning

_____ I identified who would read my paper.

_____ I identified what I wanted my paper to accomplish.

_____ I started planning my paper before I started writing it.

_____ I used a strategy to help me plan my paper.

Seeking and Organizing Information

_____ I tried to remember everything I already knew about this topic before I started to write.

_____ I got all the information I needed before I started to write.

_____ I organized all of the information I had gathered before I started to write.

Writing

_____ I thought about what I wanted my paper to accomplish as I wrote.

_____ I thought about the reader as I wrote.

_____ I continued to plan as I wrote.

_____ I revised my paper as I wrote.

Revising

_____ I revised the first draft of my paper.

_____ I checked to make sure that the reader would understand everything I had to say.

_____ I checked to make sure that I accomplished my goals for the paper.

_____ I made my paper better by adding, dropping, changing, or rearranging parts of my paper.

_____ I corrected spelling, capitalization, and punctuation errors.

_____ I used a strategy to help me revise.

_____ I reread my paper before turning it in.

Seeking Assistance

_____ I asked other students for help when I needed it.

_____ I asked my teacher for help when I needed it.

_____ I asked my parents or other people for help when I needed it.

Motivation

_____ I told myself I was doing a good job while I worked on the paper.

_____ I rewarded myself when I finished the paper.

Figure 15.6.   Sample writing process checklist.

clearly understand how to use the self-monitoring and recording procedures. Before students begin to self-monitor independently, the teacher and students should decide on a date and time to evaluate how self-monitoring is working and how the student likes it.

Step 5. Check to see whether students are carrying out the steps properly as the process is used over time. If confusion or problems exist, it may be necessary to have a short booster session to review or re-teach parts of the process. For some students, it may initially be helpful to provide a list of steps as a reminder. It is important that the student carry out the self-monitoring procedures correctly and on a regular basis. Once students have agreed to self-monitor and record, they should continue until the teacher and students agree that it is no longer necessary.

CHAPTER 16

Goal Setting

When Charles Darwin began writing his seminal work *On the Origin of Species by Natural Selection*, he had difficulty managing how much he wrote each day. Following his wife's suggestion, he stabilized his daily output by using a goal-setting strategy. Before writing, he first decided how many points he wanted to prove that day, representing each point with a pebble. The pebbles were then placed in a line on the ground outside of his study. As he proved, referenced, and buttressed each point, he kicked the corresponding pebble away.

Skilled writers use goals to help them direct what and how they write (Hayes & Flower, 1986). After reading five earlier scripts for *Star Trek II: The Wrath of Khan*, Nicholas Meyer set a goal to include certain elements from five earlier scripts written by other writers. Rudyard Kipling set a personal goal to rewrite his own work multiple times on the grounds that it could always be improved. Anthony Burgess set a goal to write 2,000 words per day after being incorrectly told that he would die within a year. He produced five books in the space of a single year!

In this chapter, we describe two validated goal-setting procedures. With the first one, a general goal for writing is established for the paper, and elaborated subgoals are established for accomplishing the main goal. Although this strategy can be applied to a variety of genres, it has only been validated empirically with persuasive writing (Ferretti, MacArthur, & Dowdy, 2000). As a result, we describe how to use it when writing persuasive essays but provide suggestions for extending its use to at least one additional genre. With the second procedure, a goal for revising is established and students are taught a strategy for accomplishing it (Graham, MacArthur, & Schwartz, 1995).

STRATEGY I: GENERAL AND ELABORATED GOALS FOR WRITING A PERSUASIVE ESSAY

With this procedure (Ferretti et al., 2000), goals are established that make clear the primary purpose of the task (i.e., take a position and persuade the reader) and specify the elements of writing needed to attain this objective (i.e., the elaborated goals). It includes the following steps:

Step 1. Before writing, the teacher asks the students to take a position on a controversial topic and write a paper to persuade their readers to agree with them (general goal).

Step 2. Before writing, the teacher also asks the students to be sure to include a statement of their belief, two or three reasons for their belief, examples or supporting information for each reason, two or three reasons why others might disagree, and why those reasons are wrong (elaborated subgoals).

Teaching the Strategy

Ferretti et al. (2000) provided few details on how they presented the general and elaborated goals for persuasive writing to students. We recommend the following steps for teaching this procedure.

Step 1. The teacher and students discuss the importance of goal setting for writing. A general goal establishes the purpose for writing the paper, helping students direct their efforts; elaborated goals focus on what they need to do to accomplish the general goal.

Step 2. The teacher tells the students that they will write a paper on a topic (e.g., "Should students be given more homework?" or "Should students go to school in the summer?"). A chart is used to present the general and elaborated goals (see Figure 16.1). The teacher checks to see that students understand what each goal means, providing clarification as needed. The teacher tells the students that meeting these goals will help them write a more convincing paper.

General Goal: Take a position on the assigned topic and write a paper that persuades the reader that you are right.

Elaborated Goals: Include

- A statement that says what you believe
- Two or three reasons that support your belief
- Examples or supporting information for each reasons
- Two or three reasons why others might disagree
- A statement about why these reasons are wrong

Writing Better: Effective Strategies for Teaching Students with Learning Difficulties, by S. Graham and K.R. Harris, © 2005 Paul H. Brookes Publishing Co., Inc. All rights reserved.

Figure 16.1.   Chart for general and elaborated goals for persuasive essays.

Tip 1: Students cannot successfully use the procedure described here if they do not understand what is meant by general and elaborated goals for persuasive writing. We recommend that teachers ensure that students know the meaning of each goal before introducing this procedure. For the parts of an essay included in the elaborated goals, we first defined each element and illustrated its meaning by examining persuasive essays written by other authors (Graham et al., 1992). Students then worked in pairs or small groups to locate these elements in other reading material, receiving help from the teachers as needed. Finally, using a topic starter (e.g., "Should kids wear uniforms to school?"), they generated their own ideas for each element until they demonstrated they understood the meaning of each of the elements captured by the elaborated goals.

Tip 2: Instead of the teacher providing feedback on students' attainment of the general and elaborated goals, students can be taught to use self-monitoring and recording to obtain their own feedback. For example, students can be taught to place a checkmark by each elaborated goal (on a recording chart) as they accomplish it in their paper.

Tip 3: Teachers may be able to increase students' motivation to attain the general and elaborated goals by having students display their overall performance on a bar chart or graph.

Step 3. The teacher assigns the topic and reminds the students to use the general and elaborated goals to write a convincing paper.

Step 4. After reading the paper, the teacher provides each student with feedback on his or her success in meeting the general goal, as well as all of the elaborated goals. Although such feedback was not provided by Ferretti et al. (2000), feedback on goal attainment is essential if goal setting is to maintain its effects over time (Locke, Shaw, Saari, & Latham, 1981).

What to Expect

This strategy was validated with fourth- and sixth-grade students with learning disabilities. Students were in an inclusive classroom, team-taught by a general education teacher and a special education teacher (Ferretti et al., 2000). As a group, their scores on an individually administered intelligence test were almost 1 *SD* below the mean (i.e., 85). Each child's writing or reading scores on a standardized, norm-referenced test was 1 *SD* or more below the mean.

When the older, sixth-grade students were asked to write two fully developed persuasive essays (elaborated goals) that would convince the reader that their thesis was correct (general goal), this procedure had a moderate to strong effect on the quality of writing (Ferretti et al., 2000). The effect size for overall persuasiveness of the first paper was .67, whereas it was .83 on the second paper. In contrast, the procedure had little to no effect on the overall persuasiveness of the papers produced by the fourth-grade students with learning disabilities. Thus, we cannot recommend its use, at least in its current form, with younger students.

Portability

The direction to write a persuasive essay that contains the basic elements of an argument (the elaborated goals) is also an effective procedure with sixth-grade students without learning disabilities (Ferretti et al., 2000). The goal-setting strategy had a moderate to strong effect on the overall persuasiveness of their essays. (Effect sizes ranged from .55 to .91.) It does not appear to be suitable for younger students, however, because it had little to no appreciable effect on the writing of fourth-grade students without learning disabilities.

This is not to say that younger students both with and without learning disabilities are incapable of meeting such goals. We have found that children as young as second grade can attain such goals after appropriate instruction (Harris et al., 2004). This instruction includes learning how to identify and generate content for the most basic elements of an argument (i.e., belief, supporting reasons, examples or elaborations, and ending) along with strategies for planning such an essay and monitoring and recording the inclusion of these elements (see Chapter 11).

Extensions

The basic idea of setting a general goal and elaborated subgoals is applicable to genres other than persuasive writing. Children with and without learning disabilities from second to sixth grades have been able to meet such goals in story writing after instruction on basic story elements, how to monitor the inclusion of these elements, and a planning strategy for story writing (Danoff et al., 1993; Graham & Harris, 1989a; Graham et al., in press; Harris et al., 2004; Saddler et al., 2004; Sawyer et al., 1992). Because students are often familiar with the basic elements of a story in the early elementary grades (Stein & Glynn, 1979), a general goal to write an entertaining story along with elaborated subgoals (tell *who, where, when, what did the characters want to do, what happened,* and *how did it end*) might also prove to be beneficial, even with students younger than sixth grade. Because this application of goal setting is untested, we recommend that teachers follow the assessment guidelines contained in Chapter 17.

STRATEGY 2: A REVISING GOAL
AND A STRATEGY FOR ACCOMPLISHING IT

This procedure involves a goal for adding information when revising the first draft of a paper and a strategy for attaining this goal (Graham et al., 1995). The steps are as follows.

Step 1. The teacher tells the students that as they revise their compositions, they need to add at least three things to improve their paper.

Step 2. The students then brainstorm at least five ideas to include in their composition to improve it, writing each idea on a separate sheet of paper.

Step 3. The students place a checkmark by the ideas (at least three) that will most improve their first draft.

Step 4. The students then decide where and how they will add the checked ideas to their text.

Teaching the Strategy

Students with learning disabilities can be taught this procedure in one or two 30-minute sessions. The strategy is taught using the following steps.

Step 1. The teacher and students first discuss why adding information, such as more detail or better descriptions, improves a paper. It will make their papers more complete and interesting.

Step 2. The teacher and students then discuss that one way to help ensure that their papers are more complete and interesting is to add information to their first draft. To help them do this, the teacher will ask them to add at least three things to make their paper better when they revise it.

Step 3. The teacher tells the students that they will learn a strategy (or trick) to help them generate good ideas to include in their composition. The teacher describes the strategy, using a chart that briefly presents each step (see Figure 16.2). The strategy includes brainstorming possible ideas to add to their first draft, writing at least five of these ideas on a separate piece of paper, placing a checkmark by the ideas (at least three) that will most improve the composition, and deciding where each idea should be added.

Step 4. Using the chart as a guide, the teacher models how to use the strategy.

Step 5. During the first session or a subsequent session, students practice meeting the goal (add three things) and using the strategy to revise an earlier composition. They are encouraged to follow the steps on the chart. (Individual charts can be made for students, if needed.) This helps ensure that the students understand

---

Goal: When revising, add three or more ideas to make your paper better.

Strategy Steps:

1. Brainstorm five or more ideas to include in your text.
2. Write them on a separate piece of paper.
3. Place a checkmark next to each idea that will make your text better.
4. Decide where and how you will add each checked idea to your text.
5. Make the revisions.

Writing Better: Effective Strategies for Teaching Students with Learning Difficulties, by S. Graham and K.R. Harris,
Figure 16.2. Chart for adding ideas to the first draft.

Tip 1: When a child was asked to name three states in which water might exist, he thought for a minute and replied, "New York, New Jersey, and Pennsylvania." We suspect that he could have named even more! Similarly, there is nothing magical about the goal to add three things to make your paper better. For some students, three things might be too much and for others, too little. The goal should be adjusted for each student so that it is challenging but attainable.

Tip 2: Some students may need additional practice to master the strategy for obtaining the revising goal. One way to provide such practice is to pair the student with another child who has already mastered the strategy. This child would act as a coach, providing help until the other child can use the strategy independently.

Tip 3: Teachers may be able to increase students' motivation to use the strategy by having them place a checkmark by each step (on a recording chart) as it is completed.

how to use the strategy and provides the teacher with the opportunity to supply any required assistance.

What to Expect

This strategy was validated with fifth- and sixth-grade students with learning disabilities (Graham et al., 1995). As a group, their scores on an individually administered intelligence test were within the normal range (mean IQ = 92). The students also experienced difficulty with writing. Their average score on a standardized, norm-referenced test of writing was 1.5 *SD below* the mean.

When the students were asked to add three or more ideas to their first draft of a personal narrative and were taught a strategy for accomplishing this objective, there was a positive change in both their revising behavior and writing performance. The procedure had a very strong effect on increasing the number of meaning-changing revisions made by students (effect size = 2.17). They made four times as many revisions that changed the meaning of text when compared with students who were told to simply revise their paper to make it better (a general goal). In addition, this shift in revising behavior had a positive impact on their writing. Their revised papers were 15 words longer than those produced by students assigned the general goal (effect size = .35). Most important, there was a strong improvement in the overall quality of their text (effect size = .87).

Portability

The value of this procedure for other students is unclear. There have been no scientific tests of its applicability beyond fifth- and sixth-grade students with learning disabilities. A case for its possible use with other elementary-age students can be made on the grounds that many students revise just like their counterparts with learning disabilities. Children in schools today do not revise frequently, extensively, or skillfully (Applebee, Langer, & Mullis, 1986; Fitzgerald, 1987). Their revisions are mostly limited to mechanical and word-level changes, and their revising behavior has little or no impact on the quality of their writing (Scardamalia & Bereiter, 1986). It seems reasonable, therefore, that setting a revising goal to add more text should also shift these students' focus to making more substantive changes in their papers. Of course, if this procedure is used with children without learning disabilities, we encourage teachers to follow the assessment guidelines contained in Chapter 17.

Extensions

What about the power of setting other types of revising goals? Goal setting is one of the most effective tools for improving performance. It has increased productivity on a multitude of academic and nonacademic tasks (Locke et al., 1979). Thus, it is likely that goal setting can be used to change other aspects of students' revising behavior. This might include setting a goal designed to increase how many revisions students make or what kinds of revisions they undertake, such as rewriting three or more sentences to make them clearer. Care must be exercised in selecting these goals. To illustrate, it is not necessarily a good idea to ask struggling writers to increase the number of deletions they make when revising a paper. We found that deletions had a negative impact on the writing of students with learning disabilities (Graham, 1997).

Extending Goal Setting More Broadly
Teachers frequently set goals for students' writing, asking them to compose a five-paragraph essay, a two- to three-page book report, and so forth. Goal setting can involve general goals, such as "write a scary story," more specific goals, such as "reference at least five sources in your paper," or product goals, such as "write a description that includes 10 interesting words."

Despite its familiarity and potential power, goal setting is not always effective. This is often because we do not properly attend to the properties of goal setting that make it effective.

1.   Goals that are specific and challenging work better than goals that are vague or easy. This is why Ferretti et al. (2000) provided elaborated goals to their rather vague goal to write a paper that "persuades the reader you are right." The elaborated goals provided a road map of what students needed to do to achieve the more general goal.

2.   Goals that can be accomplished in the very near future are preferable to long-term goals. We are all familiar with students who have a 5-week period in which to complete a term paper but do not start until a couple of days before it is due.

3.   Timely and frequent feedback is essential. It provides information on progress in attaining the desired goal, and it encourages evaluating and changing current behaviors or actions so that the goal is more readily attained. For school-age children, feedback can be obtained from either the teacher or peers, or through self-assessment.

Another important issue in goal setting is illustrated in the following scenario centered around a refrigerator. A father writes three goals for himself (help wife more, lose weight, be more productive at work) and attaches them to the front of the refrigerator with a magnet. As the week goes by, his daughter who is home from college adds, "Send Michelle money." His high school son writes, "Make car payments for Jason." Even Michelle's boyfriend get in the act, adding, "Buy Tom a jeep." The list is finally rounded out when Dad writes, "Wean kids."

Although goals assigned by others can be quite powerful, as was illustrated by the two validated goal-setting procedures described in this chapter, they must be valued to be effective (Locke et al., 1979). In the anecdote above, Dad did not accept the goals posted by his children and did nothing to make them a reality.

In school, goals can be assigned by the teacher, determined by the student, or agreed on by both parties (i.e., as participative goals). With participative goals, the teacher and the student both contribute to the selection or development of goals. For example, the student may select one or more goals to achieve from a list of goals developed jointly by the teacher and the student.

For students with learning disabilities, participative goal setting has two advantages. It has been our experience that many of these students have difficulty setting reasonable and realistic goals for themselves. We are reminded of one young man who wanted to set a goal to include 50 action words in his next story—even though his previous stories never included more than four or five action words. His teacher helped him set a more realistic objective by first discussing the feasibility of this goal and then suggesting a range of more reasonable goals as a starting point (e.g., 8, 10, or 12 action words).

Participative goals also provide needed structure for students' initial goal-setting efforts. Because students with learning disabilities often have little confidence in their abilities, the process of developing their own goals can be quite a struggle. A possible solution would be for teachers to simply tell them what they want them to achieve. However, we believe it makes more sense to make students participants in the process because this leads to perceptions of ownership and a greater level of commitment to achieve the goals. Although the eventual aim is that children set their own goals, participative goal setting provides a useful bridge for promoting this objective.

Using what we know about effective goal setting, we designed the following procedure, called SCHEME, to promote the use of goal setting for writing (Harris & Graham, 1996). This provides one example of how goal setting can be extended to play a more prominent role in writing instruction. Of course, like all other untested extensions described in this book, teachers need to carefully monitor the success of this process using the assessment guidelines in Chapter 17.

Each letter of SCHEME stands for a step in the procedure: *S* stands for skills check, *C* for choose goals, *H* for hatch plans, *E* for execute plans, *M* for monitor results, and *E* for edit.

Step 1. Skills check: The purpose of the first step is to complete an inventory of how students are currently doing. A skills check can include identifying 1) aspects of children's writing that are in need of improvement or 2) common writing processes that children fail to apply consistently (see Chapter 15, Figure 15.6, for examples). The identified skills or processes provide the raw material for developing goals for Step 2.

Step 2. Choose goals: Consistent with our earlier recommendation, this step initially involves participative goal selection. This continues until students become familiar with goal setting and how to construct their own goals. The movement from participative to independent goal selection involves three stages. First, students select goals to complete from a list of goals constructed by the teacher. Second, teacher and students work together to construct goals for completing specific writing assignments. Third, students are encouraged to construct their own goals, receiving assistance only when necessary. Once students can construct their own goals, the *C* in SCHEME is changed to "construct goals." An important point to keep in mind is that goals should be specific, challenging, and proximal.

Step 3. Hatch plans: In the third step, the plan that students will put into operation to meet their goals is specified in writing. For example, if the goal is to "write accurate directions for how to get to a specific location," a child might indicate that this will be accomplished by checking to see that the directions contain the following elements: reasons for directions, starting point, destination (both location and description), distance, mode of transportation, estimated amount of travel time, complete description of route, reference to landmarks, map, and an account of possible complications that might arise.

Step 4. Execute plans: Students execute the plans for attaining the desired goals.

Step 5. Monitor results: Progress in attaining the goals and the effectiveness of students' plans are monitored. For the task of writing directions, students should be encouraged to assess whether the directions were adequate and contained all of the basic elements. They might also be asked to consider whether their plans were used as intended and if they were effective.

Step 6. Edit: If students experience difficulty in obtaining the goals or executing their plans, actions to remedy this situation are put into effect during this final step. For example, if a child failed to include directional markers and a description of the destination for the direction-writing task, this should be corrected. The student might further decide to establish an additional goal at this point (make the directions amusing) and start the process again.

Making It Work

Daniel Walker, recognized in 1999 as a Teacher of the Year in Alaska, noted, "Teaching is brain surgery without breaking the skin. It should not be entered into lightly." We agree and think this is especially true when teaching children to be more strategic. Care must be taken in deciding which strategies to teach and how to begin such instruction.

Another important part of creating a successful writing strategies program is captured by a Teacher of the Year from Maine, Susan Niles, who counseled that the best teachers "create a safe, comfortable learning environment where students can relax and actively participate . . . [and teachers should] use lots of positive feedback and smiles to develop a sense of trust." Students are much more likely to expend the effort needed to learn and use strategies in a supportive classroom environment.

Although there is scientific evidence that each of the strategies presented in this book is effective with students with learning disabilities, such instruction is not always productive with all children. It is important that teachers make sure that writing strategy instruction works with their students. If it is not producing the expected or desired results, then instruction can be modified to make it more effective. In this final section of the book, we offer our advice for how to implement writing strategy instruction in the classroom.

CHAPTER 17

Guidelines for Implementing Writing Strategy Instruction

Advice on teaching comes in all sizes. When an 8-year-old girl was asked, "If you were president, what would you do?" she replied, "I'd change the law so there was only school from 9 to 10 in the morning." She also indicated that this hour would include recess and lunch. When it was pointed out that school would only be about 20 minutes long, she responded, "That's fine with me." In one swift legislative stroke, she made education more affordable and compatible with society's short attention span.

Rest assured, our advice on how to implement strategy instruction in the classroom does not require a major restructuring of the educational system. Rather, it involves suggestions on getting started, creating a supportive learning environment, and making sure that strategy instruction works.

GETTING STARTED

In Charles Schulz's cartoon *Peanuts*, Lucy is fond of giving Snoopy advice on his writing, urging him to write something scintillating, a blockbuster, a novel for the ages. Snoopy's response to all this advice is to bemoan the problem he's having simply writing the opening line.

The moral of this simple parable is that instead of trying to do it all at once, start at a suitable place. If strategy instruction is a new subject, begin with an existing, validated strategy (e.g., one of the writing strategies presented in this book). This is easier than designing one's own strategy and trying to become comfortable with how to teach

157

it at the same time. It is also better to start by focusing on a single strategy rather than trying to introduce several strategies at once. For example, begin by teaching students a planning strategy. Once planning is mastered, teach a second strategy such as one for revising. (Of course, the teacher could start with revising and then move to planning.) It may also be easier to begin with one of the simpler strategies (e.g., STOP and LIST) that introduces very basic processes such as brainstorming and sequencing. These processes are elements in some of the more sophisticated writing strategies, such as report writing.

The reason for advising caution on a first experience with strategy instruction is that this type of teaching may be quite different from the teacher's normal routine. If this is the case, it is not fair to either the students or the teacher to take on too much too fast. Early setbacks while teaching writing strategies can make persistence difficult for all parties.

One way to make strategy instruction more successful and satisfying is to collaborate with other teachers (Harris & Graham, 1996). This can include working with another colleague to implement strategy instruction in a specific classroom. This kind of joint effort is illustrated in Chapter 3, in which a general education teacher and a special education teacher worked together to teach the *story writing strategy* to a class of fifth-grade students. Collaboration may also involve a group of teachers who meet frequently to talk about and support their individual efforts to teach writing strategies. Strategy instruction support groups provide several advantages. They offer a forum where teachers can draw on their accumulated experience to help each other plan what strategies to teach and how to teach them. They furnish a colloquium where teachers can share and celebrate their successes and obtain suggestions on how to resolve problems that arise. Shared support may also help teachers sustain their enthusiasm and interest in teaching writing strategies.

A key principle in strategy instruction is to teach strategies that students have plenty of opportunities to use. In the letter below, Bob's teacher had clearly taught him the basic structural characteristics of a letter.

> Dear President,
>
> If you keep on doing so great, I'll bet you will probably go down in history like Rudolf the Red Nose Raindeer.
>
> Yours truly,
>
> Bob

If this was the only opportunity that this young child had to apply this knowledge, such information will be of little value and eventually forgotten. Likewise, there is little reason to teach a strategy, such as story writing, if students do not typically write stories either in school or at home.

Another cardinal principle in strategy instruction is that the number of strategies that students can learn and keep in play is limited. This principle was put to the test by our daughter who used the following strategy to study for spelling tests. Each Monday, she made a mnemonic for each word on her spelling list. She memorized the mnemonics during the rest of the week and aced the spelling quiz almost every Friday. Most of these mnemonics, and the correct spelling of many of the corresponding words, were forgotten quickly, however, as she continued to develop a new set of mnemonics week after week. The sheer number of mnemonics simply overwhelmed her ability to remember them all.

One implication of this second principle is that it is better to teach several strategies well than to try and teach every possible strategy. It is also important to sequence strategies so that they build one on the other. This helps to ensure that earlier learning does not become extraneous. Finally, it is better to teach strategies that can be geared upward and downward in terms of sophistication. This flexibility extends the life of a strategy in two ways. First, it can be upgraded so that it promotes the development of new skills and processes. Second, it can be used with a broad range of writers because it can be adapted to meet students' individual needs.

To illustrate how the implications of this principle can be actualized, we provide an example involving several of the strategies presented in this book. Our focal point for this example is students who produce little text and write without much, if any, forethought. A good starting point for these students is the STOP and LIST strategy (see Chapter 6). With this strategy, students learn how to set goals for their paper, brainstorm ideas, and sequence them. These are very basic planning skills that are central to effective writing and instrumental in the more sophisticated planning strategy we intend to teach these students later.

We would then introduce the peer revising strategy (see Chapter 7). This strategy takes advantage of peer response as a vehicle for focusing the revising and editing processes. It also provides specific criteria for evaluating both content and mechanics. One of the primary advantages of this strategy is that the number of criteria can be increased or reduced, making it a very flexible tool. Initially, we would start with only one or two criteria for both the revising and editing processes. Once students mastered these criteria, new ones would be introduced and old ones eventually eliminated when they were no longer needed. Unless it proved to be ineffective, this would be the only revising and editing strategy taught.

Next, we shift attention to genre-specific planning. The three-step strategy (see Chapter 11) would replace the STOP and LIST strategy. This replacement strategy involves three steps for planning and writing a paper. First, students identify their audience and writing goals. Second, they plan their paper by generating and sequencing possible writing ideas in the form of an outline (for a persuasive essay, they would use the mnemonic TREE). Third, they use this plan as a guide for writing but continue to upgrade and modify it as they compose.

Although there are many similarities between the three-step strategy and STOP and LIST, they differ in one very important way. The second step in the three-step strategy includes a series of prompts or questions designed to help students generate possible writing ideas for a specific genre. For example, if students learn to use the three-step strategy to write stories, the mnemonic SPACE is inserted in the second step to remind them to generate ideas for the *s*etting, characters' *p*urpose, *s*tory action, *c*onclusion, and characters' *e*motions. This feature makes the strategy very versatile, as a different mnemonic can be introduced to remind students to generate relevant content for each new genre. For example, with opinion essays, SPACE would be replaced by the mnemonic TREE, which reminds students to generate ideas for a *t*opic sentence, supporting *r*easons, *e*xamples, and an *e*nding. Likewise, a more sophisticated form of an opinion essay can be introduced by replacing TREE with DARE, a reminder to *d*evelop a topic sentence, *a*dd supporting details, *r*eject arguments for the other side, and *e*nd with a conclusion.

In this example, just three strategies are taught. One of the strategies (STOP and LIST) introduces basic planning skills, whereas the other two strategies (peer revising and three-step strategy) provide general tools that can be upgraded and modified to promote the development of new writing skills and processes. Of course, this is only one of the ways that the strategies in this book can be sequenced and combined. The correct selection and sequence will depend upon the needs of the teacher and students.

CREATING A CLASSROOM
THAT SUPPORTS STRATEGY INSTRUCTION

One of our favorite *Calvin and Hobbes* cartoons involves Calvin telling Hobbes, his imaginary tiger friend, that he has figured out how *not* to write an assigned paper. They will hop into their time machine (constructed earlier out of a cardboard box) and go a few hours into the future. Because Calvin will surely have written the story by then, they will simply collect it and return to the present, avoiding having to write the paper at all! Hobbes wryly comments that something doesn't make sense but is told to relax because they will be back as soon as they go.

When students do not value a task such as writing, they may fail to use the resources at their disposal or pursue an effective strategic solution for completing a writing assignment (Graham & Harris, 1997c). This is illustrated in a letter written by a child at summer camp:

> Hello Mom and Pop,
>
> They just told us we can't eat until we write our parents, so I am going to write enough this time to get something to eat.
>
> Love,
>
> Bud

This child's tactic was to simply get the job done as quickly and easily as possible. He did not draw on the tools or strategies he possessed because he had little investment or regard for this task.

One way to avoid such apathy (and increase the likelihood of a strategic solution) is to involve students in writing tasks that are authentic and aimed at a real audience (Graham & Harris, 1997a). They are much more likely to apply the strategies they have learned if the writing task is legitimate. This was evident in a fourth-grade classroom we observed a couple of years ago. The students had taken on the task of cleaning up a local stream. Part of this effort involved writing letters to the mayor, city council members, other influential citizens, and local newspapers. They also wrote and obtained a grant from the city government to help them clean up the stream. The children in this class were highly committed to this project, and it showed in what they wrote and what they did. They were self-directed, doing most of the work with only minimal teacher guidance. They also used the planning and revising strategies they had learned earlier in the year to complete their writing tasks.

Another way to increase the likelihood that students will apply learned strategies is to create a classroom environment that is supportive, pleasant, and nonthreatening. Children are less likely to exert the effort needed to apply a writing strategy if they view the classroom as an unfriendly, chaotic, or punitive place (Graham & Harris, 1994). Although it is true that some students are able to overcome these barriers, others evidence a mental withdrawal or evasion of productive work in such situations (Hansen, 1989).

Listed below are some things that teachers can do to make the writing classroom an enjoyable and supportive place where students are likely to use the writing strategies they are taught.

- Establish an exciting mood during writing time.
- Create a setting where students feel free to take risks when writing.
- Develop writing assignments that are compatible with students' interests.
- Allow students to select their own writing topics or modify assigned topics.
- Provide opportunities for students to arrange their own writing space.
- Encourage students to help each other as they plan, write, revise, and edit their work.
- Hold conferences with students about goals, advances, and setbacks on current projects.
- Ask students to share works-in-progress and completed papers with each other.
- Praise students for their accomplishments, effort, and use of strategy.
- Reinforce students' writing by displaying their best work in prominent places.
- Model and promote an "I can do" attitude.

It is also important to realize that placing too much attention on children's writing errors can have a negative impact (Burton & Arnold, 1963; Graham, 1982). Circling every misspelled word, red-marking each deviation from standard English, and writing "AWK" above every clumsy phrase or sentence can make students more aware of their limitations and less willing to write. In no instance should writing be used as a punishment. In the popular television program *The Simpsons*, Bart Simpson is often seen writing lines, such as "This punishment is not boring and pointless," over and over at the blackboard as a penalty for some misdeed. Using writing as a punishment is likely to promote a strong distaste for writing.

A final point about promoting students' use of the writing strategies presented in this book involves predictability. Once students are taught a writing strategy, they should be not only reminded to use it but also reinforced consistently for doing so. We also recommend that teachers establish a predictable classroom writing routine, in which students plan, draft, revise, edit, and publish their work. This provides students with plenty of opportunities to apply the planning, revising, and other self-regulation strategies they are taught.

MAKING SURE THAT IT WORKS

Not all strategies are effective. The film director Woody Allen brought this point home in his sarcastic assessment of speed-reading, a highly visible and popular strategy: "I took a speed-reading course and read *War and Peace*. It's about Russia."

Strategies that are effective with some students may not be effective with others. Although each strategy presented in this book was scientifically tested and the resulting evidence provided proof that it enhanced writing performance, this does not guarantee that it will be effective with every other child with a learning disability. Similarly, there is considerable evidence that our recommended approach for teaching writing strategies, self-regulated strategy development (see Chapter 3), is a powerful instructional model, but again this does not ensure that it will be equally effective with all teachers.

It is also important to realize that strategy instruction may have unintended consequences. For example, a child who was taught the SCAN strategy for revising persuasive essays (see Chapter 11) reduced the length of his first drafts after learning how to use this procedure. When the teacher asked him why his first drafts were now shorter, he explained, "SCAN makes me add more ideas later, so why write a lot the first time?" This student's decision to limit how much he initially wrote decreased the potential effectiveness of the strategy.

For these reasons, *evaluation* is a critical, but often overlooked, component of strategy instruction. In addition to providing confirmation that the writing strategy worked as intended with the students, evaluation is beneficial for three other reasons. First, teachers who assess closely what they are doing and how things are going are better able to take charge of the teaching process, making modifications and adjustments when needed. Teachers without such information are more likely to be controlled by the curriculum or materials they use, failing to recognize when things are not working out.

Second, ongoing evaluation of instruction provides teachers with a way of learning more about themselves and their students. Reflecting on how they and their students react during strategy instruction provides teachers with considerable insight into what they are doing and what their students need.

Third, ongoing evaluation is important for student growth. If teachers are unaware that their teaching methods are not working with some or all of their students and simply carry on without making changes, students may come to devalue the strategies they are taught. Even worse, they may interpret their lack of progress as an indication of their incompetence.

The following is a list of principles for evaluating the effectiveness of writing strategies and the procedures used to teach them. Although the list is not exhaustive, it includes principles we have found to be useful in assessing strategy instruction in the area of writing.

Principle 1. The amount of evidence collected depends on the established effectiveness of the strategy. The basic tenet of this principle is that a newly developed or untested writing strategy needs to be evaluated more closely than a strategy with a previous track record of effectiveness. This same principle applies to the methods used to teach writing strategies. Conversely, strategies and teaching methods that have been validated previously (not just by researchers but also in the teacher's classroom) need less scrutiny than newly devised methods or procedures being used for the first time. The essential point is that the amount of time and effort devoted to evaluation depends on the established validity of the writing strategy and accompanying teaching methods as well as the teacher's history with both.

Principle 2. Include students as co-evaluators. As much as possible, students should participate in the evaluation process. This not only provides them with evidence on the value of the strategy but increases their sense of ownership as well. Involving students as co-evaluators is also advantageous for teachers. It provides a practical means for reducing teachers' workloads because students complete part of the evaluation process.

One obvious way that students can participate in the evaluation process is by assessing changes in their written products. For example, if students are taught a strategy designed to increase the number of revisions they make, they can count and record how often they do this before, during, and after strategy instruction. This provides the teacher and students with evidence of the effectiveness of the strategy and the methods used to teach it.

Students should also be encouraged to evaluate their own progress during instruction. For example, they might be asked to write a journal entry (that is shared with the teacher) at critical points during instruction to consider how the process is progressing. This may include thinking about what is working well, where they are experiencing difficulty, if they need help, and so forth. Such information helps teachers judge who needs additional help and if instructional adaptations are needed.

Once students have learned to use the strategy, they can be asked to evaluate further the strategy and teaching procedures. Sample questions to ask students include

- What did you like about the strategy that you learned?
- What did you not like about this strategy?

- Did the strategy help you write better? Why or why not?

- Will you continue to use the strategy? Why or why not?

- What did you like about the procedures used to learn the strategy?

- How could we change the teaching procedures to make them better?

It is important to remember that children's evaluations are not always accurate. A young child once told Art Linkletter, the host of the television show *House Party*, that she wanted a pet beaver. When he commented that this was a rather unusual pet, she thought for a moment and rendered her own evaluation: "No, he could sharpen pencils for me." Although the accuracy of the students' assessments will need to be monitored (more so for younger children), we have been impressed with children's enthusiasm and precision when making their own evaluations.

Principle 3. Assess changes in student writing performance, behavior, and attitudes. In addition to evaluating the impact of strategy instruction on students' writing performance, it is important to see if there are corresponding changes in how students compose. The writing strategies described in this book were all designed to change how students go about the process of composing, such as increasing the amount of time students spend planning. We also expect that many students' confidence as writers will increase and that they will be more positive about writing. Thus, an evaluation that concentrates only on changes in students' written products will provide a very truncated picture of strategy effectiveness.

Remember that some changes take more time to become evident. Changes in attitude, for example, may not occur right away. Instead, such changes may occur only after students see more tangible payoffs, such as better grades or a sustained period of writing improvement.

Principle 4. Assess while instruction is in progress. Too much assessment takes place once teaching is done. Such evaluations do not provide teachers with the information they need to adjust their instructional efforts. One method that teachers use frequently to evaluate instruction on an ongoing basis is to keep a file where they jot down their informal observations on how things are going. These notes may include such things as what went well during instruction, what was problematic, who was progressing, who was having trouble, ideas for the next day, and so forth.

You can also ask each student to keep a writing folder containing the papers they develop as they are learning to use the strategy. This allows the teacher to survey their work easily and quickly in order to note progress and areas that need attention.

With the self-regulated strategy development model presented in Chapter 3, instruction is based on criteria rather than time. In other words, mastery criteria are established for each stage of instruction. For example, it might be decided that students do not move from the *Support it* to the *Independent performance* stage until they can independently use the strategy to write two successive compositions that result in a complete paper. By establishing specific criteria, teacher and students have a clear conception of what needs to be accomplished and a yardstick against which to measure progress. If the criteria are not met in a timely fashion, changes in the instructional program or the goals may be called for.

Principle 5. Assess how students actually use the strategy. Do not assume that students are using the target strategy as intended. Over time, some students will modify the strategy or how they use it. Sometimes this occurs right at the start. For example, a student might drop off a step that is deemed too hard or too easy. As time goes on, the child may further modify or drop additional steps because they are viewed as useless. Whereas some modifications may be useful, others may render the strategy ineffective.

The most direct means for monitoring students' strategy use is to observe what they do as they write. Less direct evidence can be obtained by asking them what they do as they write or by examining their papers to obtain evidence of strategy use.

Principle 6. Assess students' use of the strategy over time and in new situations. A key challenge in teaching writing strategies is students' flexible and continued use of the strategy over time. One way to determine whether students maintained what is taught is to periodically ask them to explain the purpose of the strategy and to reiterate its basic steps. If they cannot do this, it is unlikely that they are still using the strategy effectively. Students can also be asked to keep a log of each time they used a strategy and how they modified it for new tasks. This technique has the added advantage of acting as a prompt or reminder to use the strategy. You can further check to see if they use the strategy when completing relevant classroom tasks. Regardless of the assessment procedures used, the goal is to determine whether students need additional instructional support. This could include discussion of the importance of using the strategy, reminders to use it that are given during class, or specific instruction aimed at promoting more generalized use.

Principle 7. Involve other teachers in the evaluation process. When students are taught a writing strategy, such as brainstorming, that can be applied in a number of different content areas or classrooms, it is helpful to involve other teachers in the evaluation process. The aim of this principle is to determine whether the strategy is being applied successfully in these other settings. The cooperating teachers should also be asked whether the strategy is effective and appropriate for students in their classes and, if not, how the strategy can best be modified.

One of the major advantages in involving other teachers in the evaluation process is they may also be willing to help promote maintenance and generalization as well. They can be asked to remind students to use the strategy, show them how to modify it for their assignments, and provide assistance if needed.

THE LAST WORD

In case you didn't know, "There was Upper Egypt and Lower Egypt. Lower Egypt was actually farther up than Upper Egypt, which was, of course, lower down than the upper part." Although this explanation is technically correct (can you believe it?), it certainly is not very convincing or easy to read. With a bit more work either planning or revising this message, the author, a college student, could have surely done better.

This is also the central message of this book. Struggling writers, including children with learning disabilities, are capable of writing well. To do this, they need to learn how to use the same tools as good writers. The self-regulation, planning, and revising strategies presented in this book provide a bridge for these students. Although they are less sophisticated than the strategies used by professional writers, they provide a vehicle for helping students plan more effectively and become more thoughtful and reflective writers. These skills provide children with a needed window into the inner workings of the writing process.

References

Alexander, P., Graham, S., & Harris, K.R. (1998). A perspective on strategy research: Progress and prospect. *Educational Psychology Review, 10,* 129–154.

Applebee, A. (1984). Writing and reasoning. *Review of Educational Research, 54,* 577–596.

Applebee, A., Langer, J., & Mullis, I. (1986). *The writing report card: Writing achievement in American schools.* Princeton, NJ: Educational Testing Service.

Armbruster, B., Anderson, T., & Ostertag, J. (1987). Does text structure/summarization instruction facilitate learning from expository text? *Reading Research Quarterly, 22,* 331–346.

Atwell, N. (1987). *In the middle: Writing, reading, and learning with adolescents.* Portsmouth, NH: Heinemann.

Alvarez, V., & Adelman, H. (1986). Over-statements of self-evaluation by students with psychoeducational problems. *Journal of Learning Disabilities, 18,* 567–571.

Bahr, C., Nelson, N., & Van Meter, A. (1996). The effects of text-based and graphics software tools on planning and organizing of stories. *Journal of Learning Disabilities, 29,* 355–370.

Baumann, J. (1984). The effectiveness of a direct instruction paradigm for teaching main idea comprehension. *Reading Research Quarterly, 20,* 93–115.

Beal, C., Garrod, A., & Bonitatibus, G. (1993). Fostering children's revision skills through training in comprehension monitoring. *Journal of Educational Psychology, 82,* 275–280.

Bean, T., & Steenwyk, F. (1984). The effects of three forms of summarization instruction on sixth graders' summary writing and comprehension. *Journal of Reading Behavior, 16,* 297–306.

Bereiter, C., & Scardamalia, M. (1982). From conversation to composition: The role of instruction in a developmental process. In R. Glaser (Ed.), *Advances in instructional psychology* (Vol. 2, pp. 1–64). Mahwah, NJ: Lawrence Erlbaum Associates.

Berkowitz, S. (1986). Effects of instruction in text organization on sixth-grade students' memory for expository text. *Reading Research Quarterly, 21,* 161–178.

Brown, A., & Campione, J. (1990). Interactive learning environments and the teaching of science and mathematics. In M. Garner, J. Green, F. Reif, A. Schoenfield, A. diSessa, & E. Stage (Eds.), *Towards a scientific practice of science education* (pp. 112–139). Mahwah, NJ: Lawrence Erlbaum Associates.

Brown, A., & Day, J. (1983). Macrorules for summarizing text: The development of expertise. *Journal of Verbal Learning and Verbal Behavior, 22,* 1–14.

Burton, D., & Arnold, I. (1963). *The effects of frequency of writing and teacher evaluation upon high school students' performance in written composition.* USOE Cooperative Research Report No. 1523, Tallahassee, FL: Florida State University.

Danoff, B., Harris, K.R., & Graham, S. (1993). Incorporating strategy instruction within the writing process in the regular classroom: Effects on the writing of students with and without learning disabilities. *Journal of Reading Behavior, 25,* 295–319.

Dee-Lucas, D., & Divesta, F. (1980). Learner-generated organizational aids: Effects on learning from text. *Journal of Educational Psychology, 73,* 304–311.

De La Paz, S., & Graham, S. (1997a). Effects of dictation and advanced planning instruction on the composing of students with writing and learning problems. *Journal of Educational Psychology, 89,* 203–222.

De La Paz, S., & Graham, S. (1997b). Strategy instruction in planning: Effects on the writing performance and behavior of students with learning disabilities. *Exceptional Children, 63,* 167–181.

De La Paz, S., Swanson, P., & Graham, S. (1998). The contribution of executive control to the revising by students with writing and learning difficulties. *Journal of Educational Psychology, 90,* 448–460.

Diamond, J. (1999). *Guns, germs, and steel: The fates of human societies.* New York: Norton.

Durst, R., & Newell, G. (1989). The uses of function: James Britton's category system and research on writing. *Review of Educational Research, 59,* 375–394.

Ellis, E. (1986). The role of motivation and pedagogy on the generalization of cognitive training by the mildly handicapped. *Journal of Learning Disabilities, 19,* 66–70.

Ellis, E., & Lenz, K. (1987). A component analysis of effective learning strategies for LD students. *Learning Disabilities Focus, 2,* 94–107.

Englert, C., & Mariage, T. (1991). Shared understandings: Structuring the writing experience through dialogue. *Journal of Learning Disabilities, 24,* 330–342.

Englert, C., Raphael, T., & Anderson, L. (1992). Socially-mediated instruction: Improving students' knowledge and talk about writing. *Elementary School Journal, 92,* 411–447.

Englert, C., Raphael, T., Anderson, L., Anthony, H., Fear, K., & Gregg, S. (1988). A case for writing intervention: Strategies for writing informational text. *Learning Disabilities Focus, 3,* 98–113.

Englert, C., Raphael, T., Anderson, L., Anthony, H., & Stevens, D. (1991). Making strategies and self-talk visible: Writing instruction in regular and special education classrooms. *American Educational Research Journal, 28,* 337–372.

Englert, C., Raphael, T., Fear, K., & Anderson, L. (1988). Students' metacognitive knowledge about how to write informational text. *Learning Disability Quarterly, 11,* 18–46.

Ferretti, R., MacArthur, C., & Dowdy, N. (2000). The effects of an elaborated goal on the persuasive writing of students with learning disabilities and their normally achieving peers. *Journal of Educational Psychology, 92,* 694–702.

Fitzgerald, J. (1987). Research on revision in writing. *Review of Educational Research, 57,* 481–506.

Flower, L. (1979). Writer-based prose: A cognitive basis for problems in writing. *College English, 4,* 19–37.

Flower, L., & Hayes, J. (1977). Problem-solving strategies and the writing process. *College English, 39,* 449–461.

Freedman, A. (1993). Show and tell? The role of explicit teaching of the learning of new genres. *Research in the Teaching of English, 27,* 222–251.

Graham, S. (1982). Composition research and practice: A unified approach. *Focus on Exceptional Children, 14,* 1–16.

Graham, S. (1990). The role of production factors in learning disabled students' compositions. *Journal of Educational Psychology, 82,* 781–791.

Graham, S. (1997). Executive control in the revising of students with learning and writing difficulties. *Journal of Educational Psychology, 89,* 223–234.

Graham, S. (1999). Handwriting and spelling instruction for students with learning disabilities: A review. *Learning Disability Quarterly, 22,* 78–98.

Graham, S. (in press). Strategy instruction and the teaching of writing: A meta-analysis. In C. MacArthur, S. Graham, & J. Fitzgerald (Eds.), *Handbook of writing research.* New York: Guilford Press.

Graham, S., & Harris, K.R. (1989a). A component analysis of cognitive strategy instruction: Effects on learning disabled students' compositions and self-efficacy. *Journal of Educational Psychology, 81,* 353–361.

Graham, S., & Harris, K.R. (1989b). Cognitive training implications for written language. In J. Hughes & R. Hall (Eds.), *Cognitive-behavioral psychology in the schools: A comprehensive handbook* (pp. 247–279). New York: Guilford Press.

Graham, S., & Harris, K.R. (1989c). Improving learning disabled students' skills at composing essays: Self-instructional strategy training. *Exceptional Children, 56,* 201–214.

Graham, S., & Harris, K.R. (1993). Self-regulated strategy development: Helping students with learning problems develop as writers. *Elementary School Journal, 94,* 169–181.

Graham, S., & Harris, K.R. (1994). The role and development of self-regulation in the writing process: In D. Schunk & B. Zimmerman (Eds.), *Self-regulation of learning and performance: Issues and educational applications* (pp. 203–228). Mahwah, NJ: Lawrence Erlbaum Associates.

Graham, S., & Harris, K.R. (1996). Self-regulation and strategy instruction for students who find writing and learning challenging. In M. Levy & S. Ransdell (Eds.), *The science of writing: Theories, methods, individual differences, and applications* (pp. 347–360). Mahwah, NJ: Lawrence Erlbaum Associates.

Graham, S., & Harris, K.R. (1997a). It can be taught, but it does not develop naturally: Myths and realities in writing instruction. *School Psychology Review, 26*, 414–424.

Graham, S., & Harris, K.R. (1997b). Whole language and process writing: Does one approach fit all? In J. Lloyd, E. Kameenui, & D. Chard (Eds.), *Issues in educating students with disabilities* (pp. 239–258). Mahwah, NJ: Lawrence Erlbaum Associates.

Graham, S., & Harris, K.R. (1997c). Self-regulation and writing: Where do we go from here? *Contemporary Educational Psychology, 22*, 170–182.

Graham, S., & Harris, K.R. (1999). Assessment and intervention in overcoming writing difficulties: An illustration from the Self-Regulated Strategy Development model. *Language, Speech and Hearing Services in the Schools, 30*, 253–264.

Graham, S., & Harris, K.R. (2000a). Writing development: Introduction to the special issue. *Educational Psychologist, 35*, 1.

Graham, S., & Harris, K.R. (2000b). The role of self-regulation and transcription skills in writing and writing development. *Educational Psychologist, 35*, 3–12.

Graham, S., & Harris, K.R. (2002). Prevention and intervention for struggling writers. In M. Shinn, H. Walker, & G. Stoner (Eds.), *Interventions for academic and behavior problems II: Preventive and remedial approaches* (pp. 611–650). Bethesda, MD: National Association of School Psychologists.

Graham, S., & Harris, K.R. (2003a). Students with learning disabilities and the process of writing: A meta-analysis of SRSD studies. In L. Swanson, K.R. Harris, & S. Graham (Eds.), *Handbook of learning disabilities* (pp. 323–344). New York: Guilford Press.

Graham, S., & Harris, K.R. (2003b). Literacy: Writing. In R. Anand (Ed.), *Encyclopedia of cognitive sciences* (pp. 939–945). London: Macmillan

Graham, S., Harris, K.R., MacArthur, C., & Chorzempa-Fink, B. (2003). Primary grade teachers' instructional adaptations for weaker writers: A national survey. *Journal of Educational Psychology, 95*, 279–292.

Graham, S., Harris, K.R., MacArthur, C., & Schwartz, S. (1991). Writing and writing instruction with students with learning disabilities: A review of a program of research. *Learning Disability Quarterly, 14*, 89–114.

Graham, S., Harris, K.R., & Mason, L. (in press). Improving the writing performance, knowledge, and self-efficacy of struggling young writers: The effects of self-regulated strategy development. *Contemporary Educational Psychology.*

Graham, S., Harris, K.R., & Troia, G. (1998). Writing and self-regulation: Cases from the self-regulated strategy development model. In D. Schunk & B. Zimmerman (Eds.), *Self-regulated learning: From teaching to self-reflective practices* (pp. 20–41). New York: Guilford Press.

Graham, S., & MacArthur, C. (1988). Improving learning disabled students' skills at revising essays produced on a word processor: Self-instructional strategy training. *Journal of Special Education, 22*, 133–152.

Graham, S., MacArthur, C., & Schwartz, S. (1995). Effects of goal setting and procedural facilitation on the revising behavior and writing performance of students with writing and learning problems. *Journal of Educational Psychology, 87*, 230–240.

Graham, S., MacArthur, C., Schwartz, S., & Page-Voth, V. (1992). Improving the compositions of students with learning disabilities using a strategy involving product and process goal setting. *Exceptional Children, 58*, 322–334.

Graham, S., Schwartz, S., & MacArthur, C. (1993). Knowledge of writing and the composing process, attitude toward writing, and self-efficacy for students with and without learning disabilities. *Journal of Learning Disabilities, 26*, 237–249.

Graves, A., & Hauge, R. (1993). Using cues and prompts to improve story writing. *Teaching Exceptional Children, 26,* 38–40.

Graves, A., Montague, M., & Wong, Y. (1990). The effects of procedural facilitation on the story composition of learning disabled students. *Learning Disabilities Research, 5,* 88–93.

Graves, D. (1983). *Writing: Teachers and children at work.* Portsmouth, NH: Heinemann.

Greenwald, E., Persky, H., Ambell, J., & Mazzeo, J. (1999). *National assessment of educational progress: 1998 report card for the nation and the states.* Washington, DC: U.S. Department of Education.

Grobe, C. (1981). Syntactic maturity, mechanics, and vocabulary as predictors of quality ratings. *Research in the Teaching of English, 15,* 75–85.

Hansen, D. (1989). Lesson evading and lesson dissembling: Ego strategies in the classroom. *American Journal of Education, 97,* 184–208.

Harris, K.R., & Graham, S. (1985). Improving learning disabled students' composition skills: Self-control strategy training. *Learning Disability Quarterly, 8,* 27–36.

Harris, K.R., & Graham, S. (1996). *Making the writing process work: Strategies for composition and self-regulation.* Cambridge, MA: Brookline Books.

Harris, K.R., & Graham, S. (1999). Programmatic intervention research: Illustrations from the evolution of self-regulated strategy development. *Learning Disability Quarterly, 22,* 251–262.

Harris, K.R., Graham, S., & Deshler, D. (1998). *Teaching every child every day: Learning in diverse schools and classrooms.* Cambridge, MA: Brookline Books.

Harris, K.R., Graham, S., & Mason, L. (2004). [Teaching strategies for writing stories and persuasive essays: The effects of SRSD instruction with struggling second grade writers.] Unpublished raw data.

Harris, K.R., Graham, S., Reid, R., McElroy, K., & Hamby, R. (1994). Self-monitoring of attention versus self-monitoring of performance: Replication and cross-task comparison studies. *Learning Disability Quarterly, 17,* 121–139.

Hayes, J., & Flower, L. (1986). Writing research and the writer. *American Psychologist, 41,* 1106–1113.

Hendrickson, R. (1994). *The literary life and other curiosities.* San Diego: Harcourt Brace.

Hidi, S., & Anderson, V. (1986). Producing written summaries: Task demands, cognitive operations, and implications for instruction. *Review of Educational Research, 86,* 473–493.

Hillocks, G. (1986). *Research on written compositions: New directions for teaching.* Urbana, IL: National Council on Research in English.

Johnson, L., & Graham, S. (1990). Goal-setting and its application with exceptional learners. *Preventing School Failure, 34,* 4–8.

Kellogg, R. (1987). Effects of topic knowledge on the allocation of processing time and cognitive effort to writing processes. *Memory & Cognition, 15,* 256–266.

Leavell, A., & Ioannides, A. (1993). Using character development to improve story writing. *Teaching Exceptional Children, 26,* 41–45.

Locke, E. Shaw, K., Saari, L., & Latham, G. (1981). Goal setting and task performance: 1969–1980. *Psychological Bulletin, 90,* 125–152.

MacArthur, C., & Graham, S. (1987). Learning disabled students' composing with three methods: Handwriting, dictation, and word processing. *Journal of Special Education, 21,* 22–42.

MacArthur, C., Graham, S., & Harris, K.R. (2004). Insights from instructional research on revision with struggling writers. In L. Allal, L. Chanquoy, & P. Largy (Eds.), *Revision: Cognitive and instructional processes* (pp. 125–137). Boston: Kluwer Academic Publishers.

MacArthur, C., Graham, S., & Schwartz, S. (1991). Knowledge of revision and revising behavior among students with learning disabilities. *Learning Disability Quarterly, 14,* 61–74.

MacArthur, C., Graham, S., Schwartz, S., & Schafer, W. (1995). Evaluation of a writing instruction model that integrated a process approach, strategy instruction, and word processing. *Learning Disability Quarterly, 18,* 276–291.

MacArthur, C., Schwartz, S., & Graham, S. (1991). Effects of a reciprocal peer revision strategy in special education classrooms. *Learning Disability Research & Practice, 6,* 201–210.

MacArthur, C., Schwartz, S., Graham, S., Molloy, D., & Harris, K.R. (1996). Integration of strategy instruction into a whole language classroom: A case study. *Learning Disabilities Research & Practice, 11,* 168–176.

McCutchen, D. (1988). "Functional automaticity" in children's writing: A problem of metacognitive control. *Written Communication, 5,* 306–324.

McCutchen, D. (1995). Cognitive processes in children's writing: Developmental and individual differences. *Issues in Education: Contributions from Educational Psychology, 1,* 123–160.

Montague, M., & Leavell, A. (1994). Improving the narrative writing of students with learning disabilities. *Remedial and Special Education, 13,* 21–33.

Moxley, R., Lutz, P., Ahlborn, P., Boley, N., & Armstrong, L. (1995). Self-recording word counts of freewriting in grades 1–4. *Education and Treatment of Children, 18,* 138–157.

Nelson, R., Smith, D., & Dodd, J. (1992). The effects of teaching a summary skills strategy to students identified as learning disabled on their comprehension of science text. *Education and Treatment of Children, 15,* 228–243.

Nixon, J., & Topping, K. (2001). Emergent writing: The impact of structured peer interaction. *Educational Psychology, 21,* 41–58.

Persky, H., Daane, M., & Jin, Y. (2003). *The nation's report card: Writing.* Washington, DC: U.S. Department of Education.

Pressley, M. (2002). *Reading instruction that works: The case for balanced teaching* (2nd ed.). New York: Guilford Press.

Raphael, T., Englert, C., & Kirschner, B. (1989). Acquisition of expository writing skills. In J. Mason & S. Murphy (Eds.), *Reading/writing connection: An instructional priority in elementary schools* (pp. 261–290). Boston: Allyn & Bacon.

Reeve, R., & Brown, A. (1985). Metacognition reconsidered: Implications for intervention research. *Journal of Abnormal Child Psychology, 13,* 343–356.

Rumsey, L., & Ballard, K. (1985). Teaching self-management strategies for independent story writing to children with classroom behavioral difficulties. *Educational Psychology, 5,* 147–157.

Saddler, B., Moran, S., Graham, S., & Harris, K.R. (2004). Preventing writing difficulties: The effects of planning strategy instruction on the writing performance of struggling writers. *Exceptionality, 12,* 3–17.

Salomon, G., & Globerson, T. (1987). Skill may not be enough: The role of mindfulness in learning and transfer. *International Journal of Educational Research, 11,* 623–637.

Salomon, G., & Perkins, D. (1989). Rocky roads to transfer: Rethinking mechanisms of a neglected phenomenon. *Educational Psychologist, 24,* 113–142.

Sawyer, R., Graham, S., & Harris, K.R. (1992). Direct teaching, strategy instruction, and strategy instruction with explicit self-regulation: Effects on the composition skills and self-efficacy of students with learning disabilities. *Journal of Educational Psychology, 84,* 340–352.

Scardamalia, M., & Bereiter, C. (1983). The development of evaluative, diagnostic, and remedial capabilities in children's composing. In M. Martlew (Ed.), *The psychology of written language: Developmental and educational perspectives* (pp. 67–95). New York: John Wiley & Sons.

Scardamalia, M., & Bereiter, C. (1985a). Development of dialectical processes in composition. In D. Olson, N. Torrance, & A. Hildyard (Eds.), *Literacy, language, and learning: The nature and consequences of reading and writing* (pp. 307–329). Cambridge, England: Cambridge University Press.

Scardamalia, M., & Bereiter, C. (1985b). Fostering the development of self-regulation in children's knowledge processing. In S. Chipman, J. Segal, & R. Glaser (Eds.), *Thinking and learning skills: Current research and open questions* (Vol. 2, pp. 563–577). Mahwah, NJ: Lawrence Erlbaum Associates.

Scardamalia, M., & Bereiter, C. (1986). Written composition. In M. Wittrock (Ed.). *Handbook of research on teaching* (3rd ed., pp. 778–803). New York: Macmillan.

Scardamalia, M., Bereiter, C., & Goleman, H. (1982). The role of production factors in writing ability. In M. Nystrand (Ed.), *What writers know: The language, process, and structure of written discourse* (pp. 173–210). New York: Academic Press.

Schunk, D., & Zimmerman, B. (1994). *Self-regulation of learning and performance: Issues of educational applications.* Mahwah, NJ: Lawrence Erlbaum Associates.

Sexton, R.J., Harris, K.R., & Graham, S. (1998). The effects of self-regulated strategy development on essay writing and attributions of students with learning disabilities in a process writing setting. *Exceptional Children, 64,* 295–311.

Sperling, M. (1996). Revisiting the writing-speaking connection: Challenges for research on writing and writing instruction. *Review of Educational Research, 66*, 53–86.

Stein, N., & Glynn, C. (1979). An analysis of story comprehension in elementary school children. In R. Freedle (Ed.), *Advances in discourse processes: Vol. 2. New directions in discourse processing.* Norwood, NJ: Ablex.

Steward, M., & Grobe, C. (1979). Syntactic maturity, mechanics of writing and teachers' quality ratings. *Research in the Teaching of English, 13*, 207–215.

Stoddard, B., & MacArthur, C. (1993). A peer editor strategy: Guiding learning disabled students in response and revision. *Research in the Teaching of English, 27*, 76–103.

Strum, J., & Rankin-Erickson, J. (2002). Effects of hand-drawn and computer-generated concept mapping on the expository writing of middle school students with learning disabilities. *Learning Disabilities Research & Practice, 17*, 124–139.

Sutherland, J., & Topping, K. (1999). Collaborative writing in eight year olds: Comparing crossed ability fixed role and same ability reciprocal role pairing. *Journal of Research in Reading, 22*, 154–179.

Swedlow, J. (1999). The power of writing. *National Geographic, 196*, 110–133.

Thomas, C., Englert, C., & Gregg, S. (1987). An analysis of errors and strategies in the expository writing of learning disabled students. *Remedial and Special Education, 8*, 21–30.

Troia, G., & Graham, S. (2002). The effectiveness of a highly explicit, teacher-directed strategy instruction routine: Changing the writing performance of students with learning disabilities. *Journal of Learning Disabilities, 35*, 290–305.

Troia, G.A., Graham, S., & Harris, K.R. (1999). Teaching students with learning disabilities to mindfully plan when writing. *Exceptional Children, 65*, 215–252.

Washington, V. (1988). Semantic mapping: A heuristic for helping learning disabled students write reports. *Reading, Writing, and Learning Disabilities, 4*, 17–25.

Weintraub, N., & Graham, S. (1998). Writing legibly and quickly: A study of children's ability to adjust their handwriting to meet common classroom demands. *Learning Disability Research & Practice, 13*, 146–152.

Welch, M. (1992). The PLEASE strategy: A metacognitive learning strategy for improving the paragraph writing of students with mild disabilities. *Learning Disability Quarterly, 15*, 119–128.

Wong, B. (1994). Instructional parameters promoting the transfer of learned strategies in students with learning disabilities. *Learning Disability Quarterly, 17*, 73–101.

Wong, B., Wong, R., & Blenkinsop, J. (1989). Cognitive and metacognitive aspects of learning disabled adolescents' composing problems. *Learning Disability Quarterly, 12*, 310–323.

Yarrow, F., & Topping, K. (2001). Collaborative writing: The effects of metacognitive prompting and structured peer interaction. *British Journal of Educational Psychology, 71*, 261–282.

Zimmerman, B., & Reisemberg, R. (1997). Becoming a self-regulated writer: A social cognitive perspective. *Contemporary Educational Psychology, 22*, 73–101.

Zipprich, M. (1995). Teaching web making as a guided planning tool to improve student narrative writing. *Remedial and Special Education, 16*, 3–15.

APPENDIX

Sources of
Quotes and Anecdotes

Abingdon, A. (1952). *Bigger and better boners*. New York: Viking Press.

Abington, A. (1959). *Herrings go about the sea in shawls*. New York: Viking Press.

Arana-Ward, M. (1997, March 16). The lady in her labyrinth. *Washington Post Book World*, p. 10.

Asimov, I. (1994). *Asimov: A memoir*. New York: Bantam.

Brodie, D. (1997). *Writing changes everything: The 627 best things anyone ever said about writing*. New York: St. Martin's Press.

Burgess, A. (1991). *You've had your time: The second part of the confessions*. New York: Grove.

Burke, N. (1996). *Teachers are special: A tribute to those who educate, encourage, and inspire*. New York: Gramercy.

Burnham, S. (1994). *For writers only*. New York: Ballantine Books.

Charlton, J. (1997). *The writer's quotation book: A literary companion*. Boston: Faber & Faber.

Conrad, B., & Schultz, M. (2002). *Snoopy's guide to the writing life*. Cincinnati, OH: Writer's Digest Books.

Cosby, B. (1998). *Kids say the darndest things*. New York: Bantam Books.

Dexingter, R. (2000, December). *Reader's Digest*, pp. 92–93.

E-Tales two. (2001). New York: Cassell.

Friederichen, M. (2000, December). *Reader's Digest*, p. 30.

Gordon, W. (2000). *The quotable writer*. New York: McGraw-Hill.

Hendrickson, R. (1994). *The literary life and other curiosities*. San Diego: Harcourt.

Henriksson, A. (2001). *Non campus mentis: World history according to college students*. New York: Workman.

Kelly-Gangi, C., & Patterson, J. (2001). *Celebrating teachers: A book of appreciation*. New York: Barnes & Noble.

Kelly-Gangi, C., & Patterson, J. (2002). *The gift of teaching: A book of favorite quotations to inspire and encourage*. New York: Barnes & Noble.

Kuipery, R. (1995, July). *Reader's Digest*, p. 119.

Lamb, B. (1997). *Booknotes: America's finest authors on reading, writing, and the power of ideas*. New York: Times Books.

L'Amour, L. (1990). *The education of a wandering man*. New York: Bantam.

Lederer, R. (1990). *Anguished English*. New York: Laurel.

Lederer, R. (1993). *More anguished English*. New York: Laurel.

Lederer, R. (2000). *The bride of anguished English*. New York: St. Martin's Press.

Linkletter, A. (1959). *The secret world of kids*. New York: Random House.

Linkletter, A. (1962). *Kids sure rite funny! A child's garden of misinformation*. New York: Random House.

Linkletter, A. (1965). *A child's garden of misinformation*. New York: Random House.

Linkletter, A. (1995). *The new kids say the darndest things*. Ottawa, IL: Jameson Books.

Loranger, D. (2000, December). *Reader's Digest*, p. 126.

Mackall, D. (1994). *Kids are still saying the darndest things* (p. 98). Rockiln, CA: Prima Publishing.

Phillips, B. (1993). *Phillip's book of great thoughts and funny sayings* (p. 338). Wheaton, IL: Tyndal House.

Plimpton, G. (1999). *The writer's chapbook.* New York: Modern Press.

Ponder, J. (1995, January). *Reader's Digest*, p. 146.

Regan, P. (2001). *Teachers: Jokes, quotes, and anecdotes.* Kansas City, KS: Andrews McMeel.

Safire, W., & Safir, L. (1992). *Good advice on writing.* New York: Simon & Schuster.

Saltzman, J. (1993). *If you can talk, you can write.* New York: Warner Books.

Schulz, C. (1994). *Around the world in 45 years.* Kansas City, KS: Andrews McMeel.

Schulz, C. (1999). *Peanuts: A golden celebration.* New York: HarperCollins.

Sennett, F. (2003). *Teacher of the year.* Chicago: Contemporary Books.

Shatner, W., & Kreski, C. (1994). *Star Trek: Movie memories.* New York: HarperCollins.

Stone, I. (1978). *The origin.* New York: Doubleday.

Suess, D. (1941). *Pocket book of boners.* New York: Pocket Books.

Sutin, L. (1989). *Divine invasions: A life of Philip K. Dick.* New York: Harmony Books.

Trollope, A. (1946). *An autobiography.* London: Williams and Norgate.

Vonnegut, K. (1981). *Palm Sunday.* New York: Dell.

Watterson, B. (1993). *The days are just packed: A Calvin and Hobbes collection.* Kansas City, KS: Andrews McMeel.

Watterson, B. (1994). *Homicidal psycho jungle cat: A Calvin and Hobbes collection.* Kansas City, KS: Andrews McMeel.

White, J. (1982). *Rejection.* Reading, MA: Addison-Wesley.

Winokur, J. (1999). *Advice to writers: A compendium of quotes, anecdotes, and writerly wisdom from a dazzling array of literary lights.* New York: Pantheon Books.

Index

Page numbers followed by *f* indicate figures; those followed by *t* indicate tables.